THE NO RECIPE COOKBOOK

DR SAMANTHA PILLAY

THE NO RECIPE COOKBOOK

DR SAMANTHA PILLAY

samantha pillay

Copies of this book can be ordered via the author's website at
www.samathapillay.com, booksellers or by contacting:

DoctorZed Publishing
10 Vista Ave, Skye,
South Australia 5072
www.doctorzed.com

ISBN: 978-0-6489748-1-9 (sc)
ISBN: 978-0-6489748-0-2 (e)

A CiP number is available at the National Library of Australia.

Because of the dynamic nature of the Internet, any web addresses or
links contained in this book may have changed since publication and
may no longer be valid. The views expressed in this work are solely
those of the author and do not necessarily reflect the views of the
publisher, and the publisher hereby disclaims any responsibility for
them.

The author of this book does not dispense medical advice or
prescribe the use of any technique as a form of treatment for physical,
emotional, or medical problems without the advice of a physician,
either directly or indirectly. The intent of the author is only to offer
information of a general nature. In the event you use any of the
information in this book for yourself, which is your constitutional
right, the author and the publisher assume no responsibility for your
actions.

Cover design © Samantha Pillay

Printed in Australia, UK and USA

rev. date: 18/12/2020

Contents

Dedication

Dedicated to building a better future for all.

Dedicated to everyone where their past or present has hindered them being the best version of themselves.

To my son who constantly motivates me to 'upgrade' myself.

To my patients who fill me with inspiration and purpose and allow me the privilege to help them.

Foreword

A healthy diet is something that's very important to me.

In my 30-year career as an ophthalmologist, I've seen firsthand the damage wrought by type 2 diabetes. The disease is the leading cause of blindness in working-age adult Australians. Diabetic retinopathy, a diabetes complication that affects the eyes, has no symptoms in the early stages and, if it's not treated in time, can cause complete and irreversible blindness.

Type 2 diabetes is almost entirely preventable and yet the disease now affects close to one in ten Australians. Obesity is a major risk factor for the disease and one of the main ways it can be prevented, and even reversed, is through diet.

As a nation, our consumption of sugar, refined carbs and junk food is way too high. We need to cut down on sweet ultra-processed foods and get back to buying fresh, unprocessed ingredients and cooking our own food. Any initiatives that encourage the eating of real food, such as this book, should be promoted and celebrated.

As Dr Samantha Pillay points out, cooking your own food means you know exactly what's gone into it – there are no hidden sugars or other nasty surprises. You have total control.

In my medical career, I've seen so many people who simply lack the tools they need to lead a healthy lifestyle. This book will give you some of these tools.

If you don't know how to cook or just want to limit the amount of unhealthy takeaway food you eat, *The No Recipe Cookbook* could be the help you need to change your life. Dr Pillay's simple, straightforward method is easy to follow and will have you eager to get into the kitchen and start experimenting. Most of her meal ideas really are faster than ordering a takeaway and they're definitely healthier.

If this book can help even a handful of people to start cooking for themselves, it will be a step in the right direction. Let's all get into the kitchen and start taking back control over what we eat.

Your health is in your hands.

Dr James Muecke AM MBBS (Hons) FRANZCO
Australian of the Year 2020
Ophthalmologist
Chairman Sight For All

Testimonials

"While all this time cooking at home can be wonderful for some, it can be daunting and stressful, especially for all of us that are balancing busy work and life. Perfection is not the goal in the kitchen, but sustainability and satisfaction are. Everyone has a right for good and nutritious food. This is a perfect cookbook for nomads, trailblazers, dreamers, explorers, and visionaries — some quick hacks, bold ideas (a cookbook with no recipes!), and a few bigger ideas that challenge how we can think about food."

~ Nina Kurth, Technologist and Business Advisor,
Amazon Web Services, New York City,
Co-Chair, Advisory Board, The Finnish
Cultural Institute in New York

"You want something done; you ask a busy person. This no-nonsense guide to wholesome cooking has been devised by the busiest person around, single mum and urological surgeon, Dr Samantha Pillay.

Written for the busy person who wants to enjoy the simple pleasure of eating with loved ones, Dr Pillay adheres to the principles of raising children with good dietary health and sociability, as well as having children contribute to the meal itself and learning important life skills. The techniques in this book are simple and versatile which, if you follow, I guarantee the results come dinner time."

Prof Helen E O'Connell
FRACS, MD, MMed, MBBS, FAICD
Head of Urology, Western Health, Melbourne
Professor, Department of Surgery,
The University of Melbourne

"As a restaurant owner and cookbook author, I understand the importance of cooking and eating well. Basic cooking skills and the perceptions of individuals around their own cooking ability are major barriers to most people living a healthy lifestyle. *The No Recipe Cookbook* is built on the same understanding. Unlike many cookbooks, it doesn't just tell you what to do, but it explains *why* and *how.* This is fundamental to a sustainable healthy lifestyle. Healthy eating, sound nutrition knowledge, and a positive food culture are key to a healthy population and have the ability to significantly reduce the burden on our healthcare system. This book gives individuals and families the skills and knowledge they need to live a healthy life without strict rules and in a non-pretentious, relatable tone."

Themis Chryssidis, Managing Director, Sprout Food Group
M Nutr & Diet, B Psych, Cert IV PT
Accredited Practising Dietitian

"Warning: this is not your average cookbook! Not just for inexperienced cooks and those who simply don't like cooking, but also those who like the idea of halving their weekly food budget and shifting toward healthier eating. Dr Samantha Pillay has cleverly bundled her planning wisdom into an accessible, no-nonsense companion to help you learn some essential life skills. The positive effect on the family budget will have your financial adviser singing your praises!"

Chris Bray
FCA, CA SMSF Specialist, CTA
Director, Bray Chan Chartered Accountants

Introduction

Cooking – It's only a big deal if you make it a big deal.

If you're someone who enjoys browsing the cooking section of your local bookshop, looking for new inspiration, glossy pictures and recipes... put this book down immediately! It's not for you.

But if you can't cook, don't enjoy cooking, are too busy to cook, have never prepared a meal but would like to save money or lose weight by eating out less often, or you just want to be more efficient in the kitchen, this book could change your life. Learning to cook without a recipe can take the stress out of meal planning and cooking.

My Story

While I've always enjoyed cooking, my career, family life and physical limitations have meant I have never had much time for it.

As the first woman in South Australia to complete advanced training in urology to become a urological surgeon, I worked long hours in the hospital during the day and studied at night. I had no time to eat out.

In my surgical training days, there were no mobile phones or Uber Eats. For years my dinners consisted of a bowl of cereal or a microwaved shop-bought frozen meal. They were unhealthy and, more importantly, there was no joy in them. Food was simply fuel.

Then, when I became a mother, I wanted mealtimes to be about sharing good food at home. I wanted to instil good eating habits in my son and, as a doctor, I knew how important it was to eat healthily. As a single mum with a hectic full-time career, I needed a repertoire of meals that were quick, easy and stress-free.

There was also another factor influencing my need for simple meal solutions. Due to hip dysplasia that was not detected at birth, despite multiple surgeries I had a significant limp, limited mobility and hip pain that increased with age. This condition meant that the longer I stood for, the more pain I experienced. I only had a limited amount of time in the kitchen before I reached the point where I just couldn't take the pain anymore.

A trip to the supermarket could leave me in so much pain that I was unable to unpack the shopping afterwards, let alone cook a meal. Heading to the shops to buy food and then coming home to prepare a meal was not an option. It was one or the other, not both on the same day.

Sometimes, at the end of a day's work, I could hardly walk more than a few metres. My condition meant that

I had to plan all my family's meals, so everything was there, ready to go, when I started cooking.

When I finally had a hip replacement, at the age of 48, there were still years of rehabilitation before I was able to walk and stand long enough to manage to shop, unpack and cook all in one day. I found the skills I had learned stood me in good stead. The planning saved me time and money.[1] My improved mobility meant I could take on more work, so life just got busier and I had less time.

When the COVID-19 pandemic began unfolding, I became even better at planning, to the point where I only had to visit the supermarket once every two weeks to reduce my risk of exposure, which resulted in saving even more time and money. I was even able to extend the shopping to once every three weeks. This resulted in more bulk-buying, which increased my savings. I had never realised just how much one could save by bulk-buying. I found some items actually cost less when bought in larger quantities. For example, a 5kg bag of potatoes could cost less than a 2kg bag. It became a challenge to see how long I could go between shops, maximising my time and efficiency and reducing my spending. By carefully calculating costs per items to compare prices and focusing on specials, I was actually able to halve my average weekly spend for food, groceries and general household items from

---

[1]   All references to currency are Australian dollars (A$) and all measurements are metric. The barbecue I use is gas.

A$250 per week to A$125 per week. But the savings were even greater than that. On my previous A$250 per week I was eating out at least once a week. But with my two- or three-week meal planning, it was quicker and easier to eat at home.

All this has led me to develop the method I will share with you in this book. I'm going to show you how to plan and prepare easy, healthy meals with a minimum of mess. I'm going to show you how I changed my life so you can change yours.

PART ONE

WHY SHOULD YOU COOK?

Cooking is a life skill

One of the things I enjoy most is eating a home-cooked meal in my own home. Yet I am amazed at the number of people I meet who do not know how to cook, are scared to cook, lack confidence or believe it is quicker or more convenient to eat out or order in.

Eating out or ordering takeaway all the time is expensive and unhealthy and, despite what some may argue, I believe it is also more stressful and time-consuming than preparing a simple meal at home.

I believe having control over what you eat, when you eat it and how much you eat can help you gain control over your weight and finances.

You should cook at home because...
It helps prevent obesity.

As a surgeon, I treat so many patients who struggle with obesity, it can be overwhelming. Obesity impacts so many aspects of one's health and happiness.

In my personal life, the limitations on my mobility and ability to exercise have made avoiding obesity almost a full-time job.

I have always had to be mindful of what I eat. Outside of my working hours, I spend most of my time studying or working at a desk. This means it takes considerable effort to prevent weight gain and I do it by controlling what and how much I eat.

With home-prepared meals, you know your ingredients, especially the amount of salt, sugar and fats. You can enjoy simple wholefoods without high-calorie or artificial ingredients, sauces or additives. You can source fresh ingredients that will have a higher nutritional value.

In developed countries, many people today are no longer concerned about where their next meal will come from and rarely go hungry.

Instead, we have to make choices every single time we eat, and we are often faced with an abundance of options. We are also sometimes in situations where we are offered free food. Usually, these are high-calorie foods and alcohol is available too. In these kinds of situations, it's all too easy to eat and drink too much.

When you're eating out, serving sizes can be bigger than you need and it can be tempting to eat everything on your plate. Then there are the added calories of bread and butter, alcoholic or non-alcoholic drinks or dessert.

Controlling what and how much you eat and drink is easier to do at home.

It saves you money.

The cost of eating out compared to a meal at home is usually at least double. Cooking at home might save you anywhere from A$10 to A$100 per meal depending on where you eat and the number of people at your table.

If you save A$10 per meal, three times a week, that is A$1,560 a year. Work out what you usually spend in a week or a month by keeping track of all the money you spend on eating out, including drinks, coffees, snacks and alcohol. Compare this to the cost of some of the low-cost meal ideas in this book.

Work out what you could save a year. Then work out the extra savings you could make in any reduction in interest payments if you used this money to reduce your debt.

The savings you make by eating at home should easily cover the cost of this book within a week, maybe even in a single day.

It's a more enjoyable experience.

Even though I love the experience of eating out, I love eating at home even more: the house filled with wonderful smells; the sight of delicious food laid out on the table; the warmth and fun of sharing a meal with family and friends around a table.

I eat out because I want to enjoy the food, the location, the service, the total experience – not because I need to eat. I am choosing to spend my hard-earned money to treat myself, not because I have no alternative options.

If the thought of preparing a meal at home for friends, your family or even yourself fills you with dread, I hope this book will help turn it into a relaxing, enjoyable and rewarding experience. Knowing how to prepare simple and nutritious meals at home, stress-free, is a life skill everyone should have.

It's good for your wellbeing.

Taking the time and effort to do something as simple as preparing a meal, sitting down, relaxing and enjoying your food is a small luxury in our busy lives.

If I'm feeling stressed out and overwhelmed by my busy schedule, taking a few minutes to mash an avocado with a squeeze of lemon juice, salt and pepper, spreading it onto toasted homemade wholemeal bread, setting the table with a placemat, knife, fork, serviette and peppermint tea, and then sitting down to eat slowly and mindfully, does more than fill my stomach. It helps recharge my energy levels and fills my soul. That little bit of time taken to do something for me is an oasis in a day filled by service to others.

Looking after yourself by taking the time to prepare a meal or snack sends a message of self-love, which is a crucial part of self-care. The more healthy and positive things you do for yourself, the easier it becomes to avoid unhealthy habits.

If eating a piece of fruit doesn't hold much appeal, try relaxing and enjoying the process of carefully cutting the fruit up and serving it on a plate with a fork, knowing you are doing something healthy for yourself, and enjoy sitting at the table and eating it. The best food is food prepared with love and the best place to start is with yourself.

It's good for your family.

As a parent, mealtimes are a crucial part of developing and maintaining your relationship with your children and understanding what is happening in their lives. It's where they learn good eating habits, table manners, good posture, how to exchange ideas, negotiation skills and the art of good conversation. Home-cooked meals create wonderful family memories and bonds.

It saves you time.

A common reason people give for eating out or ordering in is that it saves time but if you're organised and follow my tips, you'll see this isn't actually the case.

I know what it's like to be over-worked and stressed. When I am exhausted at the end of a 14-hour day, I am too tired to go out and I am so time poor I don't even have the time to travel to and from a restaurant.

I can prepare a simple meal faster than I could get to a restaurant, order a meal and wait for it to appear, or even order and wait for home delivery to arrive.

When I'm hungry, I often can't think clearly enough to choose from a takeaway menu and when I'm mentally exhausted, I don't want to have to think about what to eat.

Having the week's meals planned in advanced reduces my stress levels so much that just writing about it and knowing what's for dinner makes me feel more relaxed.

If you want to make the person in your household who is responsible for preparing the meals stressed, just ask them, "What's for dinner?" and see how they react.

It's less wasteful.

Avoiding food waste doesn't just benefit your bank account, it's also good for the environment.

Careful menu planning reduces the amount of money you spend on food as well as waste. When I'm looking for cooking inspiration, I'll go to the pantry and fridge and look at what I already have, which means I make fewer purchases and save time and money. Using up what I already have also means I avoid having to throw out items that are past their use-by date.

When I'm planning meals, if there are ingredients I'm unlikely to use up in one meal, I plan a second meal to use the rest, especially if I'm using ingredients that don't last long, like herbs, vegetables or dairy products. I hate buying a bunch of herbs or a tub of sour cream, using half and throwing the other half out.

It allows you more autonomy and creativity.

For me, cooking is an opportunity to be creative as my work doesn't require much creativity. I think this is why I can never follow a recipe. I always want to change it by substituting ingredients, changing ingredient quantities, using only part of a recipe or combining recipes. I love the freedom of doing what I want and not following a recipe or someone else's instructions. I want to experiment and see what happens.

There is a method behind the meal that I follow, even if the ingredients vary a little each time. This approach adds variety and gives me the freedom to tailor the dish to whatever happens to be in my fridge and pantry.

Whenever I read a recipe, I immediately think of ways it could be better. It's a bit of a joke in my house because whenever I cook, after I take the first mouthful, I always say the same thing: "Next time I'll..."

The ideas in this book give you the freedom to do what you want, change them, experiment and create your inventions.

When you cook, your choice of what to eat is not limited by a takeaway menu. When you make healthy choices, you are in control. If you don't cook because you don't like following a recipe or following someone else's instructions, you'll need to learn to cook without a strict recipe.

It's better than a meal-delivery kit.

These days, meal-delivery kits, where you are sent the ingredients and recipe cards, are popular for those with limited time who want to eat healthy, fresh food.

But these kits can be expensive and, while the recipes can be easy to follow for novice cooks, you still have to follow a recipe and you're still limited to a menu.

If you cook at home, using my method, you'll have total control over what you eat.

It's good for your self-confidence.

Some people don't cook because they are anxious about the result of not being good enough. With no recipes and no glossy pictures of perfect-looking dishes, this book can give you the courage to cook, take risks and experiment. I enjoy taking risks when I'm cooking. Unlike in my work as a surgeon, if it doesn't work out, it doesn't matter.

MY TIPS & TRICKS

Here are some of my tips and tricks to help you make cooking simple and stress-free.

Cut down on the washing-up.

If you don't want to cook because you think it takes too much time to clean up afterwards, the key is not to make a mess in the first place. Cook in a tidy and organised way and clean up as you go.

There are also several tricks I use to minimise the amount of washing-up.

Measure in the mixing bowl: To avoid using a separate cup or bowl for measuring ingredients, if it's possible, I just place the mixing bowl directly onto the kitchen scales. I then zero the scales and add the ingredients directly to the bowl. This may mean having to convert a cup to millilitres or milligrams. But, with my time-management obsession, I have to admit I would rather guess the quantity than use, wash and put away an extra utensil! The more experience I have with making a particular dish, the more I can just transfer the ingredients straight to the pan or bowl without even measuring them. The meals I describe are suited to this method of cooking as the quantities can be varied according to your creativity and taste and the availability of ingredients.

Re-use utensils: When I cook, I think about the order I will be measuring the ingredients in. For example, if I'm using a cup to measure, I will use it first for dry ingredients, like rice, so that it doesn't need cleaning before re-using it to measure stock. I would also use a teaspoon to measure baking powder before measuring vanilla extract. I will chop the first lot of ingredients for a meal on a board, add them to the saucepan and, while they are cooking, use the same board to chop the next batch of ingredients to avoid using a second board. (However, you should use a separate board for meat, especially chicken, to avoid transferring bacteria to other ingredients). These small automatic steps add up so that I don't finish cooking and have a huge mess to clean up.

Use a barbecue: Barbecuing food, especially meat, outdoors on a grill is a great way to save on washing a frying or grill pan. I love how quickly my gas barbecue heats up.

Wash up as you go: As I cook, I stack dishes in the dishwasher, do any handwashing that's required, put away ingredients as I finish with them and wipe down surfaces. By the time I finish cooking, there is usually minimal cleaning up required.

Delegate the rest of the washing-up: Delegate doing the dishes to the rest of the family you are cooking for.

Delegate tasks to the whole family

A key part of good time management is delegation – and this doesn't just extend to the dishes. It's easier for one person to take over the responsibility for all the meal preparation than it is to delegate because delegating isn't easy.

Delegation is a skill and it takes practise to acquire it, but the effort can pay off in the long run.

Small children are quite capable of helping in the kitchen. It teaches them responsibility and life skills and is a starting point for one day cooking for themselves. Knowing how to feed yourself is an essential skill.

You can start by involving them in meal planning.

Meal planning: Getting your kids involved in planning the week's meals gives them an understanding of your role and the effort it requires. It also teaches them time management, decision-making and planning skills. It means there's less chance of hearing that annoying question: "What's for dinner?" because you all know. It can also help avoid battles at the table with fussy eaters because they've already agreed to the week's meal plan.

Meal preparation: Even small children can help to get out the ingredients, put them away, clear up, stack the dishwasher as you are cooking and set the table. As children get older, they can help with chopping, washing and stirring. It can be an enjoyable time spent together.

Invest in good kitchen appliances and equipment

I use several kitchen appliances and equipment that I refer to throughout this book. Some are expensive items that require a significant upfront investment and will take a long time to recoup, such as breadmaker and coffee machines. But you can keep these big items in mind for occasions where friends and family might join together to buy you a gift.

Breadmaker: For my 50th birthday, I asked my family to all buy me a breadmaker. Even if you use a bought bread mix in the machine, you can make a good-quality wholemeal loaf for about A$2 instead of paying A$4 for a supermarket loaf. This saves us A$2 every week.

The savings will vary considerably depending on whether you buy ingredients in bulk, whether you buy a premixed product, where you shop and how many loaves you make per week, but the savings add up over the years. And if making fresh bread at home means you are more likely to make a sandwich for lunch instead of buying it, there will be even more savings.

Coffee machine: I used to buy my coffee out every day – and not just one, sometimes up to four a day.

But since buying a coffee machine over ten years ago, I rarely buy a coffee. The savings in one day alone are significant and just continue to add up over time. It does take time to recoup the initial cost of the machine, but you can buy one second-hand. Besides, you don't spend as much time queuing and waiting for your café coffee order.

Slow-cooker: This is a great time saver – set and forget a one-pot meal with minimal washing-up. Several of the meals I describe use a slow-cooker and they freeze well.

Egg poacher and waffle maker: A big cooked Sunday breakfast is an excellent home tradition. There can be a significant saving if you cook it at home rather than eating it out. If you're anxious about cooking, learning to master breakfasts is also a great way to start and I have given several breakfast ideas in this book. We regularly use an egg poacher and a waffle maker; neither are expensive purchases compared with a café breakfast or brunch every weekend.

Mini herb spinner: I thought my salad spinner was amazing until I acquired a mini-spinner for herbs. I probably use this more than my salad spinner.

Cook on the weekend

Time management is probably the main reason I cook on the weekends. On Sunday mornings, I'm full of energy. In addition to preparing a cooked breakfast, I often bake bread and biscuits or slices for school recess for the week. I'll prepare double batches of pancakes, crêpes or waffles to freeze for school-day breakfasts. I might also start some of the preparation for Sunday night dinner in the morning and prepare a sandwich filling for school lunches. I'll often do an extra-slow-cooker meal just for freezing for weeknight dinners. I might make a pesto or curry paste to freeze for a quick weeknight meal or I'll make enough patties to freeze for two easy weeknight dinners. If you take them out of the freezer in the morning, patties will defrost quickly in the fridge by evening.

Tips for entertaining

Sharing food with friends at home can be more relaxing than going out if you take the stress out of the food preparation. Keep it simple, so you have time to enjoy yourself. Don't make life unnecessarily difficult by setting your goals too high. If you can develop a few easy, go-to options from the ideas in this book, your confidence will grow.

Work with lists: When I entertain, I always work with lists of what needs to be done and the order in which they need to be done. I carefully plan the menu so that I don't need to do several things at the same time and prepare what I can in advance.

Tips for shopping

Stick to your list: In addition to preparing meals at home, the other main way to save money and time is to have a shopping list you stick to. This limits food waste and unnecessary purchases.

Order online and keep track of expenses: Unscheduled purchases are more likely to be unhealthy and high in calories. It's very tempting to buy food to consume immediately, either at the shops, on the way home or when you're unpacking the shopping. Try this exercise. Calculate how much you spend in a month on your food shopping. Then, using a shopping list, ask someone else to do the shopping for you or order online to avoid the unscheduled purchases and calculate your savings. There are various apps available to help you keep track of your expenses. Once you start counting every dollar you spend shopping, it becomes easier to resist those unscheduled purchases.

SAM'S KITCHEN SAFETY TIPS

My years working in the emergency department as the surgical registrar on call made me very safety conscious. If you never learned to cook as a child, you may not instinctively think about the things that others take for granted and you may not know about kitchen safety.

If you are starting out in the kitchen, here are some of the things I've learned:

1. Using the electric mixer, blender or food processor: When you're finished mixing or blending, as well as turning off the appliance, turn off the power at the power point before you open the lid. Add ingredients or scrape down the bowl and replace the lid before turning the power on again.

2. Wash graters with a cloth only in one direction, away from the cut edges. Wash knives using the cloth over the top blunt area, never from the sharp edge.

3. Don't drop sharp utensils like knives in the sink so they're hidden under soap suds and then search for them with your hand. Keep them on the bench and hold them in the sink

while you wash them, then put them out to drain.

4. Use a knife block on the benchtop or in the drawer. Don't leave sharp knives lying in the drawer, to be felt around for.

5. When chopping, if you push down, place your hand only on the top of the knife on the blunt edge, so if you slip, you can't cut your hand.

6. Never cut onto your hand or fingers. Always use a chopping board.

7. By keeping the knife tip in constant contact with the board, you can move the rest of the knife up and down to avoid slipping with the blade as you cut.

8. Use the claw grip: Curl the fingers of the hand that is holding the ingredients so the knife moves up and down with your knuckles against the top, blunt part of the blade rather than your fingertips. The classic cook's knife has a broad blade.

9. There are safety gloves available that offer some resistance to cutting and are worn on the hand without the knife, while you're holding the item you are cutting.

10. Don't leave food on the stovetop unattended, especially when heating oil. Take care to stand back when adding ingredients to hot oil, which may splatter.

11. Make sure saucepan handles face the outer side edges of the stovetop so they are not over other hot plates and hobs or sticking out from the front of the stovetop, where they could get knocked.

12. Use proper heat-resistant oven mitts for handling anything hot, not a folded tea towel or, worse, bare hands. When opening the oven door, stand back, looking partly away, and let the initial heat rush out before bending down and peering in.

13. Jewellery, especially long necklaces, can get very hot when bending down to an open oven, causing an unpleasant surprise when you stand up.

14. Be careful of flammable clothing and tie back long hair. Hair spray and other products make hair highly flammable.

15. Turn off the heat when you finish cooking and move the pan to a hot plate or hob that wasn't used and serve or remove the cooked food. Wait for the pan to cool before moving it. Transfer pans and trays directly from the oven onto the stovetop above rather than walking through the kitchen to a bench or sink with a hot pan. When using the barbecue, serve straight from the barbecue to plates or another dish and leave the hot dish on the barbecue, turned off while you eat. Remove it when cool.

16. When cooking pasta, I prefer to use a pasta saucepan, which is a double saucepan with an inner colander. Once the pasta is cooked, you lift the inner colander. This can be done at the stovetop and the pasta can then be transferred straight into the pan with the sauce. Alternatively, the whole pan can be transferred to the sink and the colander lifted there and placed on the draining board. Either way, the pot of boiling water can then be left to empty when cooled.

17. Don't lick sharp knives.

18. Don't taste hot food; let it cool.

19. Don't cook in bare feet, your underwear or naked. Wear clothing that offers some protection.

20. When lifting the lid on a hot pan, tilt the steam away from you.

21. Use extreme caution when handling hot oil or making jam, candy or toffee. These hold a much higher heat than boiling water and will stick to the skin.

22. Keep a fire blanket and fire extinguisher in the kitchen or very close by.

23. Do a basic first-aid course.

PART TWO

MEAL IDEAS

Faster than takeaway!

The following meals and ideas demonstrate how I plan for 14 days of evening meals from the one supermarket shop.

I have grouped some days and meals together. For example, chicken stew, soup and ragu are grouped together on days 4 and 5 as the ingredients required are suitable to use on days 4 or day 5 after shopping, but they can be used earlier or later if your ingredients have been stored well. I've given some ingredient substitutions to allow you to alter when the meals are prepared in your shopping cycle. For example, some risotto options can be made with freezer ingredients, allowing you to move this meal to any time in week two.

It is by using the freezer and pantry-item meal options, combined with some frozen, prepared meals, that I have been able to extend my supermarket trips to every three weeks. As you become confident with the meals and variations, you will be able to vary the meals so that each two weeks are not the same and you can make substitutions to allow the meals to be used on alternative days to the ones I have suggested.

Meal planning tips

Week One – Freshest first: Plan the meals for the first two days around the freshest ingredients with the shortest shelf life, such as green, leafy vegetables and fish. The next few days are planned still using fresh ingredients, but those with a longer shelf life, such as potatoes, carrots and chicken, which you can use within four days, or beef, which you can use within five days.

Week Two – Long-life last: Vacuum-packed cuts from your butcher like lamb or pork shoulder will keep for a week, to use for a slow-cooker meal the following weekend. In week two, I might focus on eggs, tofu, frozen vegetables or tinned tuna.

You can gain a few extra days before you need to shop by using frozen ingredients and having a store of previously prepared, frozen meals.

Make double quantities: Making double quantities when you're cooking meals and freezing half means there is a second meal for week two in your menu plan. If a meal doesn't freeze well, consider making double quantities and having the same meal for two consecutive nights. Fried rice doesn't freeze well but is fine refrigerated and reheated in the microwave the next day.

Smart storage: It's worth researching the best ways to store the ingredients you buy, to get the maximum life out of them, with the minimum waste. If I buy ingredients with a short expiration date that I might not use all of in a single meal, I will plan other meals to use what's left. For example, if I buy a bunch of parsley, I might plan to use it in a pasta sauce, a risotto and a stew over three days.

Ideas for using leftover herbs and garnish

- Chop leftover herbs, mix with garlic and butter and freeze for up to two months in an ice-cube tray. Use on bread, steak or to add to a dish at the end of cooking.
- You can freeze leftover lemon zest, juice, wedges, slices and even whole lemons.

How to store herbs

- Trim the base of the bunch of herbs and place them in a glass with a small amount of water in the bottom.
- Cover the herbs with the plastic bag they came in or a freezer bag and change the water daily.
- Some herbs, like basil and mint, will do better if you loosely wrap them with paper towel, sprayed lightly with water, before covering with the plastic bag.

Celery leaves - the magic garnish: Next time you use celery, don't cut off the top leaves and throw them away. Wash and dry them, lay them on absorbent paper towel, spaced out, in the microwave. Cover with another paper towel. Microwave on 30-second intervals until crisp and dry but still bright green, not brown.

Alternatively, you can dry them in the oven or a dehydrator. Store in a dry, airtight container. They add great flavour and can be added to soups, stock, casseroles and risotto. You can mix some with salt to make your own celery salt to add to salads and sandwiches. One bunch of celery will have enough leaves for several months' supplies. Celery is often fresher when sold as a whole bunch than in individual stalks.

Chilli: I buy a bag of fresh chillies in bulk, as they keep well in the freezer in a zip-lock bag. I just take out what I need, cut them while still frozen and add to cooking without needing to defrost.

Ginger: Again, you can, of course, buy fresh ginger, but it's also available in bags, frozen, shredded and packed into individual cubes, which I love as it is so quick to add to dishes without the hassle of peeling and chopping. The cubes defrost quickly while I'm getting things ready and they defrost even faster if they're cut while still frozen.

Garlic: I like to keep my fresh garlic in the freezer as well. I break up the garlic bulb into cloves and freeze, unpeeled, in a zip-lock bag. They are much easier and quicker to peel frozen than fresh.

Buy a vacuum food sealer: This is another great gadget that allows you to remove the air and seal food in plastic bags. It's a great way to pack food for freezing as items take up far less space. The bags can be stacked straight into the freezer without using a container or worrying about messy leakage. You can use a simple hand pump rather than an electrical pump. It's more affordable and takes up less space.

Freeze in flat layers: Food frozen in thinner layers will also defrost faster. If I buy a packet of beef mince and place it in the vacuum bag, I flatten it out with a rolling pin before vacuum sealing and freezing.

Similarly, patties frozen in a single layer rather than stacked will be ready to defrost quickly in the fridge and won't stick together. These bags can be washed and reused, but each time you cut off the seal and re-seal, you will make the bag smaller.

Grow your own veggies: The coronavirus pandemic has encouraged more people to start home vegetable and herb gardens in response to fears over the disruption of food supply chains, to minimise the risk of virus exposure from shopping trips and to reduce their living costs. Even growing one fresh herb at home, like parsley, will mean you can use it in many dishes. It will mean you have a constant supply of it and save you having to buy it. Drying herbs out in the oven, microwave or food dehydrator will allow you to store them longer.

EVENING MEALS

Cookbooks traditionally start with breakfast and then move through lunch and dinner, then on to desserts and baking. But this isn't a traditional cookbook. I am starting with the evening meal as this is where the most savings can be made in terms of money, time and calories.

The evening meal is the main meal for most households. Australians often refer to this as 'dinner' or 'tea' and the English call it 'supper'. Whatever you call it, the evening meal is where people are most likely to eat out, order takeaway or use a meal-delivery service.

DAY 1

OPTION 1: STIR-FRY – FAST & FURIOUS

Choosing stir-fry early in the shopping cycle makes the most of using your freshest vegetables with the shortest shelf life first. A stir-fry cooks quickly, but the preparation takes time, so make sure everything is ready to go once the cooking starts. Fresh stir-fried vegetables should still be crisp. The trick is not to overcook the ingredients.

People often think making a stir-fry is easy, but working with heat takes skill. It is essential to get the cooking times and pan temperature right – there is little room for error or you will overcook or burn the fresh ingredients.

If the pan temperature is too low, there is too much moisture from wet ingredients, you have overcrowded the pan or added too many ingredients too quickly, you won't get crisp, tasty vegetables with some browning on the outside, but a soggy, limp mess instead.

Stir-fry is best when eaten straight away. Think of those great Asian restaurants where you hear the sizzling wok and the food is brought straight out as soon as it is cooked. Call the family to the table when you are about to start cooking and have the rice ready. Work fast and furious and enjoy the adrenaline rush – it's good for learning how to work under pressure and great if you need some excitement in your day!

The heat: Heat the pan on a moderate-to-high setting. The pan is hot enough when you drop a little water into it and it spits, sizzles and disappears. Take the time to allow the pan to heat up before you start cooking.

Equipment: Using a wok means you can move your ingredients around quickly so they don't burn. The classic wok is steel, round-bottomed and light so it heats up and can be moved around quickly. Stainless steel will also have these advantages. Heavier materials may take longer to heat up or reduce the heat and are heavier to move around. Non-stick surfaces may not tolerate high temperatures.

Oil: Don't use olive oil or butter, which will burn. Instead, use an oil with a high smoke point like peanut, sunflower or canola oil. If the oil is smoking, you will have very little time to avoid burning the food.

Working with heat: The high heat helps to brown the ingredients quickly. Adding the next lot of raw ingredients cools the pan down, so you can use this to prevent overcooking or burning the ingredients that are already in the pan. But adding too many ingredients too quickly, or adding wet ingredients, can cool the pan down too much.

The base of the wok is hotter than the sides, so cooked ingredients can be moved up the sides of the wok and the next ingredient added to the centre. With experience, you can master the key points that will influence cooking times and pan temperature. These are the size you cut the ingredients, whether they are fridge or room temperature, the volume or quantity added to the pan and the order in which ingredients are added to the pan. You will be able to move the ingredients around the pan and cook the meal in a few minutes. When you're starting out, you can even remove ingredients from the pan and add them back later.

The ingredients:

The great part is you can use a wide range of fresh ingredients – any combination of the list below. I have listed the ingredients in the order that I would usually add them to the pan, although it may only be a matter of a few seconds and stirs between additions, depending on how hot the pan is and how finely you've chopped the vegetables. Similarly, the order in which I add the ingredients might vary based on the chunkiness of the chopping and the quantity or freshness of the ingredients.

Don't be limited by this list. Experiment and learn from your mistakes. You can cook meat or other ingredients in batches and add them back later if you need to. You might need to do this if you have large volumes, so you can brown the meat and not crowd the pan and have too much liquid or a drop in temperature. When you're starting out, you may do this just to give yourself more time. Getting that browning on the outside of the meat adds flavour.

My suggested ingredients, in order of cooking, are:

- Chopped onion.
- Lemongrass – thinly slice the white part of the stalk after removing the outer leaves, base and tops.
- Chopped or grated ginger and garlic.
- Thinly sliced beef or pork fillet or chicken cut into bite-size pieces, or seafood – this is even easier to overcook than beef or

chicken. You can cook this first and add it back in later.

- Chopped chilli.
- Cubes of marinated, firm or fried tofu (not silken or soft as this will fall apart).
- Fresh baby sweetcorn (can be cut in half lengthways).
- Sliced carrot – thin rings will cook very fast, thicker are slower.
- Green beans.
- Broccoli cut into florets or smaller – pieces small enough to fit in your mouth.
- Sliced capsicum.
- Sugar snap peas.
- Snow peas.
- Spring onions (add these earlier if they are large pieces).
- Sliced bok choy, cabbage or Chinese cabbage.
- Tinned water chestnuts or bamboo shoots – drained and chopped.

Noodles: You can serve stir-fry with rice or noodles. If I am adding noodles, I would add them after all the above ingredients, so they heat through before I add the sauces. You can use dried or fresh noodles. Dried noodles need to be soaked in boiling water and drained first. Fresh noodles are usually stored in the fridge and added straight to the pan. Shelf-fresh noodles are great to have on hand in the pantry. They are like fresh noodles and are added straight from the packet to the wok at the end of cooking. They are packed in individual serves and don't need to be refrigerated.

Sauce: Next, add the sauce. If you add it too early, the liquid is all gone by the end, leaving a sticky mess on the bottom of the pan. Adding it just before serving allows you to use the liquid to extract any yummy flavours in the brown stuff off the bottom of the pan. Experiment with different sauce combinations. Don't cook the stir-fry for too long with the sauce or all the liquid will be gone and the ingredients will be overcooked.

Some sauces you could try are:

- Dark or light soy sauce, or both.
- Chilli or sweet chilli sauce – vary amounts to your taste and whether you have already added fresh chillies.
- Oyster sauce.
- Hoisin sauce.
- Kecap manis – this sweet Indonesian soy sauce is good when cooking for kids. Be careful not to add it too early or the sugar will cause a sticky mess in the pan. You can substitute it with sweet chilli sauce, brown sugar or palm sugar.
- Dark sesame oil. Just add a small amount at the end. It has a lower smoke point than light sesame oil, so if added earlier, it will burn and lose its flavour.
- Rice wine vinegar.

A good starting point might be equal quantities of dark soy and hoisin sauce.

Now you can turn down the heat and, if you need to, take a deep breath.

Final ingredients: These are ingredients you can add at the end that don't need cooking, just mixing and heating through:

- Fresh bean shoots.
- Fresh herbs like basil or coriander.
- Nuts like peanuts or cashews or sesame seeds. These can be dry-roasted or toasted beforehand in the wok without any oil at a lower heat and set aside until the end.
- Shredded omelette. Cook beaten eggs in the wok on a medium heat, before cooking any other ingredients (except nuts), tilting the wok so the egg spreads to the sides of the wok. Cook until set and then flip. Don't worry if it breaks when you flip it as you will cut it up into strips to add back into your stir-fry at the end of cooking.

Pantry stir-fry: Although I have listed stir-fry as an ideal meal to prepare soon after shopping to maximise the use of fresh ingredients, there is a version that can be made from long-life and frozen ingredients in week two. For a 'pantry' stir-fry, I use onion, garlic, ginger and chilli from the freezer (see Meal Planning Tips, page 30). Frozen chicken or beef can be thinly sliced and even added straight to the hot wok while still frozen. You can also try marinated or fried firm tofu and tinned whole baby sweetcorn, bamboo shoots or tinned whole baby mushrooms.

There are similarities to the ingredients and methods for fried rice, which I describe on page 80. For stir-fry, I will chop the ingredients into larger pieces, such as strips of capsicum and whole sugar snaps or snow peas, but for fried rice, I chop the ingredients much smaller. I will also often have fewer ingredients in my stir-fry.

Leftovers: If you have leftovers you want to save, transfer these to a storage container straight away. If you leave the food sitting in the hot wok, it will continue to cook even if you have turned off the heat and removed the pan from the stovetop. Stir-fry doesn't freeze well but you can have the leftovers the next day for lunch or dinner.

OPTION 2: FISH CAKES

Fish cakes are a great healthy meal. I like to use fresh fish fillets but you can easily use a can of tuna instead and make this recipe later in the week. I like to cook fresh fish within one to two days of buying it.

The fish: A firm, boneless white fish is a good option. In Australia, this might be gurnard or cod, or in the UK, haddock. Salmon fillets will add a richer flavour. You can also use smoked fish, like salmon, or a combination of smoked and cooked fresh fish for a less intense flavour. Any leftover cooked fish can be used. If I'm using tinned tuna, I prefer tuna in spring water. You can also leave cooked fish fillets in the fridge for another couple of days before making the fish cakes.

Freezing: If you're freezing the fish cakes, I prefer to freeze them before coating with egg and breadcrumbs and cooking them.

Potato: I use mashed potato as the main ingredient to hold the fish cakes together. Floury potatoes, like Desiree or King Edward, are best for mashing. I use approximately equal amounts of fish and potato. I prefer my fish cakes not to be too fishy, so I might even use more potato, with a ratio to fish of 2:1, which means a smaller amount of fish goes a long way.

Step 1: Start to boil a large saucepan two-thirds full of water with the lid on while you peel the potatoes. Once peeled and chopped, add the potatoes to the water and bring to the boil.

Note: It doesn't matter if you add the potatoes to the water before starting to boil, partway before the water is boiling or once the water is boiling. These variations will just determine the time it takes to cook them. The smaller the pieces of potato, the quicker they will cook. Cut one potato into about six equal-sized pieces. If you cut the pieces too small (or in uneven sizes), the potato, or at least some pieces of it, will be more likely to overcook and fall apart.

The potato is ready when a skewer or fork passes through the soft potato easily but with mild resistance and without breaking the piece.

Step 2: Drain the potatoes and transfer to a large mixing bowl or jug. Mash the potatoes with a potato masher, for speed and ease, until they are smooth and fluffy. If you over-mash them they will become rubbery and glue-like.

Step 3: Cook raw fish fillets in a pan with some oil and melted butter. The fillets are cooked when the colour changes to opaque and they break apart easily. You can use the same pan to cook the fish cakes without cleaning it. If you can multitask, you can usually cook the fish fillets in a frying pan in the time it takes for the potatoes to boil in the saucepan. Transfer the cooked fillets to a plate. When cooled, flake into pieces with a fork and add to the bowl with the mashed potato.

Step 4: While the fish is cooling, prepare the other ingredients and add them to the bowl in any order you like.

Ingredients you can add include:

- Sliced spring onions.
- Frozen or fresh peas.
- Corn kernels – frozen, tinned or fresh, cooked and then cut from a cob.

For flavour, I like to add a combination of lemon zest, chives, parsley, capers, a teaspoon of mustard and a heaped dessert spoon of mayonnaise. I find I don't usually need to add a beaten egg to my fish cake mixture. If you add an egg or lemon juice and the mixture is too wet, the fish cakes are more likely to fall apart, so I prefer to squeeze the lemon juice over at the end.

Another great flavour combination is chopped chilli, finely sliced kaffir lime leaves, lime zest and coriander with a splash of fish sauce. You can vary the quantities of these ingredients to your taste, but remember, you still want the main ingredient to be the mashed potato to hold the fish cakes together.

Step 4: Mix everything to combine evenly and shape into patties using your hands. Don't make the fish cakes too big as they will be more likely to break when you turn them over.

Step 5: Beat one egg (more if needed) in a wide, shallow bowl. In another bowl, place panko breadcrumbs. Dip each fish cake in the egg and let the excess drip off before placing them in the breadcrumb bowl and coating with breadcrumbs. Place each fish cake on a tray or plate and refrigerate for at least half an hour before cooking. This helps to prevent them from breaking apart during cooking. They can be prepared to this point in the morning so they only need a few minutes of cooking in the evening.

Step 6: Fry the fish cakes in a pan of melted butter on a medium heat so the outside is golden brown and the fish cakes are heated through. Serve with lemon or lime wedges and a salad or even on their own.

OPTION 3: PAN-FRIED FISH FILLETS

If this all sounds too hard, try a simple meal of pan-fried fish fillets. Cook the fillets as described for the fish cakes and serve them with lemon wedges and either a salad or mashed potato and microwaved frozen peas.

Mashed potato: To make the mashed potato, mash some cooked potatoes as described for the fish cakes before adding butter, salt and pepper and mashing slightly more to combine without over-mashing.

Salad: The simplest salad is to place washed and shredded lettuce leaves in a bowl with a sprinkle of sea salt. Then drizzle just enough olive oil to lightly coat the lettuce when it is mixed together, but not so much that it pools in the bottom of the bowl. Then add a sprinkle of vinegar. The ratio of oil to vinegar is 3:1. Use the best quality olive oil and vinegar you have. You can try some of the different flavour-infused vinegars, or try balsamic or white balsamic vinegar.

OPTION 4: Baked-fish PARCELS

Baking fish is another excellent healthy, straightforward way to cook fish. There are various flavour combinations you can use, depending on your taste and the type of fish you buy.

Baking fish in a moderate oven can give you time to do other things. A moderate oven might be 180 degrees Celsius, but in my oven, it is about 160.

Baking paper parcels: Cooking *en papillote* in French or *al cartoccio* in Italian is a method of folding a paper parcel with the fish and other ingredients inside so it steams and cooks in the oven. It saves on washing-up and is a lovely way to serve the dish, but for some, it is daunting and fiddly. But for me, using paper means you don't need any expensive baking dishes. Alternatively, cook in an ovenproof baking dish with a lid. You want to minimise the amount of liquid that escapes, so if your lid has a hole for steam to escape, cut a piece of baking paper to cover the dish and then put the lid on top of the paper. Place the fish and all other flavourings in your baking dish or paper parcel and bake. There are plenty of YouTube videos to demonstrate how to fold the paper parcels.

The fish: Choosing which fish to use will depend on what is available and fresh. There are plenty of options and a good fish shop should be able to advise you. You can use a soft or firmer fish.

Flavour option 1

Lemon juice, lemon zest, capers, dill, butter, sea salt, ground black pepper, shallots, garlic. You can vary the amounts of each depending on your own taste. Personally, I love strong lemon flavours. Capers can vary in quality and taste, and rinsing is recommended before using. Shallots are milder than onion and require less cooking. (I much prefer these in salads to raw or even red onion). Garlic can overpower the subtle flavours of the fish if you use too much. I love garlic but this is one dish where I will only use one clove and crush it in the garlic press to get finer pieces.

Flavour option 2

Lime (juice and add zest if you want more lime flavour or finely shredded kaffir lime leaf), chilli, coriander and lemongrass. If you want a richer sauce, you can add some coconut cream. With coriander, you can use the roots as well as the leaves for flavouring. I remove the hairy bits on the roots and just throw the white parts in, but make sure you remove before serving. Pull the leaves off the stems and add to the dish just before serving. But make sure you wash them to remove the unpleasant gritty crunch of any soil. Different chillies have enormous variations in heat intensity and have less heat if you remove the seeds. Lemongrass has excellent flavour but also needs to be carefully washed. To save time, you can just slice in half lengthways, throw it on top of the fish and remove it just before serving.

Cooking time: How long you cook the fish depends on how many pieces there are and their size and thickness. It might take 10-30 minutes. You can check every 10 minutes by taking them out and using a knife to cut into the thickest part. When done, the flesh should be soft, opaque and separate easily. When under-cooked, the flesh is firmer, slightly translucent and hard to separate.

Sides: The delicious juices from this dish work well served with bread, rice or potatoes - boiled, steamed or mashed. For a healthier option, serve with quinoa or brown rice.

Veggies: Serve with steamed or pan-fried vegetables such as peas, spinach, asparagus, beans or carrots for option 1 or Asian greens like bok choy for option 2.

To pan-fry bok choy, remove the base, separate the leaves and wash thoroughly. Cut the green leaves from the flatter, paler stems. Roughly chop the stems into a few pieces. Melt butter over medium heat in a frypan and add chopped garlic when the butter is foaming. Fry the garlic until it softens and smells delicious. Add the stems first. They will only need a few minutes to heat through, then add the leaves, which may only need a minute to wilt and heat. Serve immediately.

OPTION 5: SALMON PASTA

Salmon works well fried, baked or poached. It is a richer and oilier fish, so I prefer to balance it with ingredients like lemon, salt, capers and dill rather than butter, cream or oil. I prefer to poach salmon first as this avoids adding oil and removes some of its natural oiliness. I then flake it and add it to a pasta sauce. The plain pasta helps to balance the richness of the salmon. For the sauce, I fry shallots and garlic with a little butter in a non-stick pan, then deglaze with verjuice and add the flaked salmon, capers, dill, salt and pepper. Mix through cooked pasta and serve.

Poaching fish: Poaching is a great way to cook fish or chicken. The principle is to cook it in water or stock. You want to cover your fillet with water but I would heat the water first. I usually use a deep frying pan (or sauté pan) but a saucepan will do. Place the fillet in the pan and cover with water – then remove the fillet. Add any herbs you like, such as bay leaves, peppercorns, lemon, lime and even some onion or carrot. The important thing is the liquid should not boil. The water should be shaking as if it is about to boil. You will need to watch it to make sure the temperature is right and adjust the heat during cooking to prevent boiling. I heat the liquid to the point where it is shaking before adding the fillet back to the water. Alternatively, if the water starts to simmer with fine bubbles, I will add the fillet, which will drop the temperature, and I then turn the heat down slightly.

Deglazing: Deglazing the pan is a method I refer to in several recipes. When food such as meat, but also onions and other vegetables, are fried, provided the pan is hot enough and there is not too much liquid, a chemical reaction occurs between the proteins and sugars. This causes the ingredients to brown. The brown substance on the bottom of the pan has a rich, caramel-like flavour that will enhance the taste of your meal. If you add liquid to the pan it will lift this substance off the pan. This is called deglazing. It makes cleaning up easier. Note: if the pan is too hot, the food and pan will blacken from burning, which will taste bitter.

DAY 2
OPTION 1: BEEF MINCE

Mince is less expensive than other beef cuts and is easy and quick to cook. This is a great Day 2 choice because I like to cook mince soon after buying it. Alternatively, raw mince can be frozen and then defrosted in the fridge for 24 hours before using. This allows you to make mince dishes later in your shopping cycle. Buy the best-quality beef mince you can afford. These dishes are versatile, low cost can be made in large quantities and they freeze well.

SAVOURY MINCE

Try starting with this simple recipe. It has a sweetness that appeals to children. It can be served with rice, pasta or bread, on toast or in a toasted sandwich.

Tacos: You can also serve it in tacos. It tastes better and is healthier than a packet sauce mix and you know exactly what your ingredients are. Add shredded lettuce, sour cream and mashed avocado. If you're making this later in the shopping cycle, with defrosted frozen mince and long-life taco shells from the pantry, you may not have fresh lettuce or avocado. In this case, you can sprinkle chopped, dried celery leaves (see Meal Planning Tips, page 30) or parsley on top of your taco mince.

Another fresh ingredient you can add to your tacos, particularly if you're making these the week after your last shop, is fresh sprouts. Sprouts and microgreens are nutrient-rich and can be grown without soil on trays or in commercially available sprouters that sit on your kitchen windowsill.

This method makes a savoury mince with a small amount of thick sauce. You can vary the amount of sauce according to your taste.

You can add whatever vegetables you like in whatever quantities you like, but make sure you chop them in small pieces, so all the ingredients look a similar size, rather than having small pieces of mince with large pieces of vegetables.

Step 1: Heat a heavy-based saucepan on medium heat. If you allow a heavy-based pan more time to heat up before you start cooking, you will be able to use a lower heat setting. Add oil, but if the oil is smoking, your pan is too hot.

Step 2: Fry some chopped onions until translucent and add chopped garlic until soft and aromatic. If the onion or garlic turns dark brown, they are burning and will taste bitter.

Step 3: When you add the mince, you want the meat to brown nicely. I therefore usually turn up the heat before adding the mince. If the pan is overcrowded, it isn't hot enough, or too much liquid comes out of the mince, it will stew rather than brown. The browning of the meat adds flavour. I will use the largest pot I have or start by browning the mince in batches, removing it and setting aside, then adding it back to the pan once I have cooked the onions and garlic.

Step 4: Add some diced vegetables, beginning with those that require the longest cooking times, like carrot and celery. Celery adds depth of flavour and should be cooked well. After these vegetables soften, I might add peas and corn kernels. They can be fresh, frozen or tinned.

Step 5: Turn down the heat to maintain a low simmer.

Step 6: For easy flavour, add some tomato ketchup. Use about half a cup of ketchup for half a kilo of mince and add a heaped dessertspoonful of soft brown sugar. Tomato ketchup usually has vinegar, which is balanced by the sugar. Although ketchup already contains sugar, the extra sugar can make this a sweet treat.

If you use tomato sauce instead of ketchup, you might not need the sugar as there is usually no vinegar in tomato sauce.

If you prefer a dry mince, leave out the tomato ketchup and sugar and cook until the liquid evaporates. If you want more sauce, add extra liquid in the form of tinned tomatoes, passata, tomato paste or stock. If you end up with too much sauce, just keep cooking it down until the liquid is reduced to your desired quantity.

Adding some red wine or verjuice as the first liquid to deglaze the pan adds some acidity. Brown sugar can be used to balance the acidity. Play around with the combination of acid, sweet and salt to suit your taste.

Step 7: Add a tin of rinsed red kidney beans and a dash of Worcestershire or Tabasco sauce if you like.

Savoury mince is a great dish for beginner cooks. It doesn't matter if you overcook it as long as it doesn't burn on the bottom of the pan.

PASTA BOLOGNESE

Bolognese sauce is a great classic, with variations around the world that probably bear little resemblance to its traditional Italian origins. Perhaps calling this an 'anything and everything goes' pasta sauce would be more appropriate. If your version is simply stewed mince and a tin of tomatoes, I urge you to experiment with building more flavours and vegetables into your sauce. Be creative and adventurous.

This is a variation of the savoury mince above. Long

cooking times can build flavours. Starting with more liquid that is reduced over time will intensify flavours.

This can also be left to cook in a slow-cooker, but then less liquid is used as the liquid won't reduce much over the cooking time. My freezer is always packed, so I cook a large pot of Bolognese over a few hours so that I am left with very little liquid and very intense flavour. I then freeze it in meal portions as the Bolognese base sauce. When using it later, after defrosting, I add a tin of tomatoes or some passata to add volume and liquid to create more sauce.

Step 1: If you would like to add bacon or pancetta, fry this first in a little oil until it's as crisp as you like. Drain on paper towels and break or cut into small pieces to add back later. Then brown the mince in batches, remove and set aside.

Step 2: Cook the onion and garlic in oil and butter.

Step 3: Add mince and any juices that have drained. Deglaze the pan with some red wine, verjuice or beef stock. You will only need half a cup of liquid. As you stir the liquid in, it will lift off the flavours stuck to the bottom of the pan.

Step 4: Add chopped chilli (if you like) and diced carrot, celery, capsicum, green beans and peas. You can vary the vegetables and quantities to your taste. Use what is in season, fresh, on sale or sourced from your local community or own garden.

For extra flavour, add finely chopped anchovies. I am not that keen on eating whole anchovies but when dissolved into this dish they melt away and add flavour. You only need a couple. Good-quality anchovies are an expensive optional addition to an otherwise affordable meal.

Step 5: Add the other liquid to make up your sauce. Use one heaped spoonful of tomato paste per tin of tomatoes and/or tomato passata, plus a dash of Worcestershire sauce. If I have homemade frozen veal stock cubes, I will add one or two of these. Add the cooked bacon if using.

You can also add sliced kalamata olives. You can add herbs such as bay leaves, oregano and thyme.

Oregano and thyme are easy-to-grow perennials. Just cut, wash and add the twigs with the stems. This is much easier than trying to remove the leaves, which will fall off during cooking. At the end of cooking, just remove the twigs and bay leaves from the pan and stir in chopped fresh parsley.

Step 6: When serving with pasta, I prefer to use spaghetti, cooked so it still has some bite. It is important not to overcook it especially as I prefer to mix it with the sauce in one pot so the pasta is coated before serving.

OPTION 2: MEAT AND VEG

The classic meat and vegetable dinner is an easy go-to meal: your choice of lamb, pork, beef or veal with your choice of vegetables. It could be used anywhere from Day 2 to Day 5. Fresh meat will keep refrigerated for up to five days. So, for example, you could serve lamb with carrots, peas, mashed potato and gravy on day 2 after shopping and beef with beans, pumpkin and cabbage on day 5. How long your vegetables keep when refrigerated will depend on the quality and freshness of the products you buy. Note fresh bread, baked on Day 2, can be served with the evening meal and again with Days 3-5. If you have leftovers, this can be frozen for toast or used to make breadcrumbs and fried crusts (see below or see page 60).

The meat: A good butcher will be able to advise on what meat is good quality and fresh and how to cook it. Good-quality meat, cooked perfectly, needs no marinating. In Australia, we are blessed with access to fabulous-quality meat. Good-quality meat can be expensive. When buying expensive cuts, use small portions and serve with plenty of vegetables and bread or carbohydrates. Save the large quantities of meat for the large cook-ups of mince or slow-cook cheaper cuts.

Grilling: Good-quality cuts only need to be lightly rubbed with oil and salt before cooking. I love using the barbecue outside. In most parts of Australia, our climate is mild enough to allow this all year round.

Grilling meat on the barbecue saves on washing-up. I have a hooded gas barbecue, so I make sure the temperature is high first, to help seal the meat, and then I turn it down when I add the meat. And how do you cook to perfection? Using a meat thermometer takes out the guesswork. Add the meat to the hot grill and close the lid. Turn only once. After turning, add the meat thermometer and cook to the desired temperature. Lamb is best cooked medium-rare to rare. Ideally, remove meat from the heat before it gets to the desired temperature and wrap in foil to rest. The temperature will continue to go up a few degrees. A good meat thermometer will allow you to select the type of meat and the degree of doneness and will even notify you when to stop cooking and start resting just before it reaches this temperature.

My favourite splurge is a lamb rack or beef fillet. Serve lamb with mint jelly and beef with mustard to avoid the extra work of making gravy.

Vegetables: Adding plenty of vegetables to a small portion of lean meat is a healthy meal option. Good options include carrots, potatoes, pumpkin, green beans, peas, brussel sprouts, cauliflower or cabbage. The classic 'meat and three veg' might seem like too much effort. Who wants to clean up a pan for the meat and another three pans for the vegetables? I eliminate one pan by cooking the meat on the barbecue. Three vegetables can be cooked in one pan by adding them at different times, depending on their cooking times.

Cooking veggies: With a little practise, it won't take you long to get perfectly cooked vegetables. Overcooked vegetables are too soft and lose flavour. Vegetables should still have bite and crispness and retain their bright colour. Steaming and boiling are good options but I prefer not to boil my vegetables in water as I feel I lose too much flavour.

I find the quickest option is to cook in a frypan with just a small amount of butter and water. This is called glazing. Add about two-parts water and one-part butter to a deep frypan that's large enough for all your vegetables. Once the butter melts, whisk with a fork into the water. Use enough butter and water to cover the base of the pan in a shallow layer. Most of the liquid should be gone by the time the vegetables are cooked.

Think about the times it takes to cook each vegetable and the sizes of the pieces you have chopped. I might have carrot cut into batons or circles that I will add to the pan first. They may only need 1-2 minutes before adding green beans and then, after a couple of minutes, fresh peas. The total cooking time may only be 5-6 minutes.

Green vegetables like beans, broccoli and asparagus turn bright green when they are done and will start to lose their brightness if you overcook them (in addition to going limp). Spinach cooks so quickly that leaves can be added to the pan after you turn off the heat and there will be enough heat in the pan to wilt them.

The simple taste of a small amount of butter is enough to allow the flavour of the vegetables to shine. I use salted butter. After cooking, you can add more salt, butter or chopped fresh herbs. If you're using garlic, it should be minced or chopped finely and added at the beginning before the vegetables.

Potatoes: Mashed potatoes will require using another pan. Boiling and mashing potatoes are described under Fish cakes in the Day 1 section on page 42.

You can add salt, butter, ground pepper, chopped parsley or chives, milk or cream. Small baby potatoes are good because they don't need peeling.

You can serve them whole and even cook them in advance and then reheat by adding them to you butter-water mixture in the frypan as the first vegetable.

Fried crusts: These can be served with any meal as an alternative to bread, crisps, chips or garlic bread. If you usually throw away the crust on a loaf of bread or cut the crusts off your sandwiches, keep them in a bag in the freezer. Then defrost, cut into batons and fry them in a pan with melted butter and chopped garlic.

DAY 3
RISOTTO - Slow & Steady

Risotto is a great family dish to have in your repertoire. It is so flexible that once you master the basics you can just vary the ingredients according to your taste and whatever you have in the kitchen.

It is a pleasure to stand at the stove, stirring, bringing together the flavours, especially if it means opening a bottle of white wine for the dish and enjoying a glass while you cook. Though I have found that making risotto can be just as enjoyable and relaxing without a glass of wine, using verjuice to deglaze the pan instead. For me, stirring the pot is a relaxing time out of my busy day.

I generally find risotto doesn't freeze that well, but I still make larger quantities because of the time it takes to prepare it. It is still reasonable quality reheated in the microwave the next day and we don't mind having the same dish for two consecutive nights.

The rice: It is essential to use risotto rice (Arborio or carnaroli rice). It takes longer to cook but gives a creamier result. If you just overcook long-grain rice it will become mushy, not creamy. There are several different rice brands. I recommend getting to know a particular brand as the amount of liquid required varies with the brand, but I never bother measuring the quantity of rice or liquid. I just keep gradually adding the liquid until it starts to look cooked and then taste it to see if it's cooked.

The equipment: This dish suits a heavy-based pan for slow-cooking on a lower heat, which allows you to build flavours and deglaze the pan.

The ingredients: Different groups of ingredients work well together but you can use whatever combination takes your fancy.

Example - Mushroom risotto

I use a selection of different mushrooms, depending on what is available at my local fruit and veg shop. I like to be able to see good-sized slices of mushroom in my dish, which also means less chopping is required.

Using a few dried porcini mushrooms adds a stronger flavour and they are easy to have on hand in the pantry. The water you soak them in can be added to your stock. I usually use chicken stock. Squeeze the liquid out of the soaked porcini mushrooms and cut them into smaller pieces.

Other ingredients: You can also add garlic, onion and fresh herbs like parsley or thyme. For a more substantial meal, you can add bacon or chicken. Use the best parmesan you can afford. The secret to a great risotto is: when the rice is just cooked, add grated parmesan, salted butter, sea salt and freshly ground black pepper to taste. The quality of your chicken stock will also impact your final result. There are some good packet stocks available. If you're organised, make your own stock next time you have roast chicken (see Chicken stock, page 104) and freeze it.

Step 1: I like to fry my mushrooms first in butter with a few sprigs of thyme. You don't want too many mushrooms at a time, otherwise they stew in the butter as they release moisture. Instead, you want to create that lovely brown on the outside. This might mean pan-frying the mushrooms in batches. I first melt the butter on a lower heat until foaming, to avoid the butter browning too quickly. I then turn the heat up when I add the mushrooms. If you use a separate pan to fry the mushrooms, once they are set aside, make sure you deglaze the pan with some wine, stock or water to get all the flavours from your mushroom pan, and add it to your risotto dish later. (Note: Fried, buttery mushrooms with thyme can also be eaten on toast for breakfast or as a light meal.)

Step 2: Set the cooked mushrooms aside, then add oil and butter to your risotto pan on a low to medium heat. You want the butter to foam but not turn brown. Add the chopped onion and garlic. You can vary the quantities according to your taste, but for one cup of rice, I use one brown onion and four cloves of garlic. I prefer to use onion rather than shallots as their flavour is too subtle and becomes lost in this dish. I prefer to add the onion first and allow it to go translucent before

I add the garlic, otherwise the garlic is easily burnt. You don't want the onion or garlic to turn brown, which will happen if the pan is too hot, but the pan should be hot enough to hear a sizzle when you add the onion. No sizzle means the pan is not hot enough and spitting means it is too hot. Test by adding a few pieces of onion first. If your pan is too hot, turn off the heat and wait a while. Allow the time for the pan to heat up slowly on a low to medium heat. I can tell when the onion and garlic are perfectly done when I smell the beautiful aroma of cooked onion and garlic.

Step 3: Add the risotto rice. About one cup will use roughly one litre of stock and serve two adults. Heat the rice until the outer part goes more translucent and the centre part is still white. It is now ready for that first splash of acidic liquid. You can use half a cup of white wine and this will deglaze the pan – stir to lift off all the yummy flavours stuck to the bottom of the pan. If you don't want to open a bottle of wine, try verjuice. You could also use lemon juice or 'tomato water'. **To make tomato water,** just pulse ripe tomatoes in a blender. Put in a pan, add some sea salt and warm gently but do not boil. Then place in a fine-mesh strainer lined with cheesecloth. The resulting liquid is like water with a red tinge. You could even use it instead of stock to cook the risotto.

Step 4: Once the acidic liquid is absorbed, start adding the stock slowly, one to two ladles at a time. The stock should be warm, just simmering, so you need it on the stovetop in another saucepan. I sometimes heat the stock in a glass jug in the microwave to near boiling and reheat along the way if required. Stir the stock in and, when absorbed, ladle in some more. The process of gradually adding the liquid allows the starch in the rice to be released slowly and results in the creaminess. The process usually takes about half an hour.

Step 5: When the rice is half cooked, I start adding my other pre-cooked ingredients, like mushrooms, bacon or chicken, and then the fresh ingredients, like fresh peas. When the rice is cooked, it will have a glossy, creamy coating and be firm but soft to bite, not crunchy. If you run out of stock towards the end you can just use some water, but adding too much will give a watery taste. As a short cut, you can just add chopped, raw mushrooms halfway through cooking the risotto, and you will still end up with a delicious meal.

Step 6: When the risotto is just cooked, turn off the heat and add finely grated parmesan and salted butter and stir through until melted. This will make it even creamier. You can also stir through finely chopped flat-leaf parsley and add sea salt and pepper to taste. I like to add a lot of grated parmesan (about one-third of a cup) and a good slice of butter (20-30g for one cup of rice). Adjust to your taste.

In summer, serve with a simple lettuce salad (see Salad, page 46).

More risotto ideas

There are other ingredients you can cook first to add flavours to the pan and set aside to add back later.

Chicken risotto: If you use chicken, thigh fillets are tender and flavoursome and you can cook them for longer than chicken breast, which will be tougher when overcooked. I cut the fat off my thigh fillets, which is tedious, time-consuming and not a job I enjoy. To save time, I often use a good free-range organic chicken breast cut into bite-size pieces. By cooking this first in your risotto pan, setting aside and adding it back to the risotto towards the end of cooking, the chicken is beautifully tender, rather than tough and overcooked.

The brown bits stuck to the pan will add flavour to your dish when deglazing. If you're cooking the chicken first, the key is for the pan and oil to be hot enough so it will brown, as this gives the delicious flavours. You want the pan at about 140-160 degrees Celsius before you add the chicken.

If you burn the bottom of the pan, don't deglaze this – just use another pan for your risotto. If you add too much chicken to the pan it will stew rather than brown as there will be too much moisture, so it is best to cook it in batches if needed. You at least want all the outside cooked, with some lovely brown areas.

Eventually, you need the chicken to be cooked all the way through to kill bacteria. If you take the chicken out when it's fully cooked on the outside but not cooked all the way through, you will need to add it back to your risotto earlier for further cooking than if it is cooked all the way through. You can check how well-cooked it is by cutting one of the pieces in half. When cooked, it should be white all the way through with no pink or translucent bits, but still tender and juicy. When you add it to your risotto, add back any juices that have been released while resting. After cooking the chicken, turn off the heat before you start the risotto as you want the pan at a lower temperature for the risotto than for browning the chicken.

Bacon: As with the chicken, if you're cooking the bacon first, you can fry it until it is crispy, then add it back later and use those lovely flavours in the pan. Again, you need the pan to be hot enough and to cook the bacon in batches. A medium heat should be enough to cook both chicken and bacon. After I cook the bacon, I rest it on absorbent paper to reduce the oils before adding it back later.

Vegetables: Risotto is a dish you can adjust to your tastes. If you don't like mushrooms, leave them out. Chicken and bacon go well with peas, broccoli, lemon juice, lemon zest, toasted pine nuts and leeks. You could even try asparagus or cabbage. If I use leeks, I caramelise them first by cooking them in butter and a little oil. Add other fresh vegetables towards the end to avoid overcooking. The size you cut your vegetables will also affect their cooking times. Caramelising leek or onion takes a long time. I prefer to do it in the slow-cooker as I add them sliced with a small amount of butter and leave them to cook for about eight hours on low heat. A large batch can be made up this way and then frozen in portions to use later.

Cabbage risotto: This can be a very affordable meal as a whole cabbage is much cheaper than meat. I cook the shredded cabbage separately in foaming butter in a very large pan before adding to the risotto as it cooks down to a much smaller volume. You could also add raw cabbage halfway through cooking the risotto but you then need a larger pan to cook the risotto in.

Saffron risotto: A generous pinch of saffron added after deglazing the pan, when you start adding the stock, is all you need, then finish off with parmesan, butter, salt and pepper. Although saffron is expensive, with this simple dish you save on other ingredients.

Seafood risotto: Seafood is expensive and you don't want to overcook it. For a prawn risotto, make a risotto with onion, garlic, fish stock or tomato water, and you can also add chilli, parsley, lemon juice, lemon zest or peas. Pan-fry the prawns or other seafood separately in butter until cooked through and stir through at the end to avoid overcooking.

Other meats: Other meat ingredients you can try include pan-fried pancetta, sliced chorizo or spicy sausage.

Roasted pumpkin risotto: Roast cubed pumpkin and pine nuts first in the oven. Add near the end of cooking the risotto and serve topped with crumbled goat's cheese and rocket.

Pea puree and fried pancetta risotto: Add both of these near the end of cooking to keep the bright green colour of the peas and the crispness of the fried pancetta. Try adding lemon zest, garlic and parsley. For an easy pea puree, boil frozen peas in salted water for 3 minutes, strain and puree in a blender for a couple of minutes, adding a spoonful of the cooking water to loosen. For a smoother finish, strain it by pushing it through a fine seize with the back of a spoon.

Turkey risotto: Try frozen leftover turkey with Swiss brown mushrooms and garlic, onion and truffle salt.

Pantry risotto: You can also make the following risotto from only pantry and freezer items in week two. The day before I make it, I transfer a frozen chicken breast and a portion of caramelised leeks to the fridge to defrost.

I then cut the chicken cut into bite-size pieces and brown in oil on moderate heat. Then I remove the chicken from the pan and turn down the heat. I then make the risotto the same way as the steps above. About halfway to two-thirds through cooking, I add back the chicken, then the leeks. Once heated through, I add frozen peas. You can also defrost a whole frozen lemon, zest the lemon, and add the lemon juice instead of the verjuice, and the zest when you add back the chicken.

Enjoy being creative and try something different every time.

DAYS 4 & 5
OPTION 1: CHICKEN STEW

There are several variations and combinations of flavours that use chicken and vegetables to create a one-pot dish. This style of cooking saves on washing-up and is less stressful, especially when you're already multitasking in your everyday home life. This dish freezes well so I always make double quantities.

Chicken cuts: I prefer to use chicken breast or thigh fillets. As with risotto, if I'm using chicken breast, I will cook the chicken first in batches, remove it from the pan and add it back later to avoid overcooking it. Cooking chicken pieces with bones will add even more flavour. Buy the best quality chicken you can afford such as free-range, grain-fed chicken.

Sides: The chicken stew can be served alone or with bread, rice or pasta. I like cooking the rice in the microwave as it means you only need to manage one pot on the stove.

Pie: Chicken stew can also be used as a pie filling, either with pastry or topped with mashed potato. Pies can be frozen, although freezing the chicken stew in portions to use later in a pie usually takes up less room in the freezer.

Sauce: The amount of chicken stock you add, and the length of time you cook the dish to reduce the liquid will determine the amount of sauce you have at the end. If you want a thicker gravy, lightly coat the chicken pieces in plain flour, seasoned with salt and black or white pepper, before frying.

There are many good chicken stocks available, although they are quite expensive compared with the cost of making your own (See Chicken stock page 104). Chicken stock freezes well and is used in many dishes.

Step 1: Start by heating a heavy-based pan on a moderate heat with oil.

Almonds: If I am going to add almonds at the end, I dry-fry slivered almonds or almond flakes in the pan first, without oil. They will burn quickly once they start to brown, so stir constantly and remove them quickly, starting with a lower heat if you need to. They will be very hot, so transfer to a dish to cool before touching or trying them.

Bacon: If I'm adding bacon, I cook it first – I like it crispy – and set it aside to add at the end. You can also use leftover chopped ham instead of bacon. Bacon can be stored in the freezer, with plastic wrap or baking paper between the slices.

Step 2: Fry the chicken pieces (dusted in seasoned flour if you want a thicker sauce). Have the heat high enough and fry in batches, so they brown but don't burn. Remove the chicken and set aside. Don't worry if bits of chicken are stuck to the bottom of the pan.

Step 3: Turn down the heat if you need to, add a little butter and fry chopped onion until soft and translucent, then add garlic and fry until soft and aromatic. You can also use shallots but they are more expensive and their milder flavour can be lost in this dish.

Step 4: Fry your selection of chopped vegetables. I usually add the following in the order listed, but you can use any combination you like. Allow enough time to fully heat through each ingredient before adding the next one, but not enough time to cook it completely.

- Leeks (unless you're adding frozen caramelised leeks, in which case you can add them later).
- Diced carrot and diced celery.

Step 5: Next, deglaze the pan using anywhere from a quarter to half a cup of liquid, there's no need to measure it exactly. You can use verjuice, white wine or chicken stock. More stock can be added here and throughout the cooking until you reach the amount of sauce you prefer. This liquid will also lift off all the stuff stuck to the pan that you thought was going to be a nightmare to clean off. You can add back your chicken and bacon or ham now or later, depending on whether further cooking is required and how many more ingredients you have to add. Add any juices released from the resting chicken. The chicken should be fully cooked through.

Step 6: Other vegetables can be added next, including green beans, mushrooms, corn, peas and fresh, frozen or dried porcini mushrooms. Dried porcini mushrooms need to be soaked in hot water first for 5-10 minutes (see Mushroom risotto, page 62), drained, chopped and added together with the liquid they were soaked in. Although they're expensive, you only need a small amount to add flavour and they last up to a year. I will sometimes fry the mushrooms first in butter, after I've fried the almonds. Quite a bit of moisture comes out of mushrooms when you cook them. Frying them in batches on a higher heat helps to brown them.

Step 7: Flavours that go well with chicken can be added next, including mustard and lemon zest. You can add some cream if you want a creamy sauce. Use double cream with at least 48% fat, which helps to stop the cream separating when it's boiled. Bring to a simmer and serve when the vegetables are cooked. Add lemon juice, tarragon or parsley towards the end of cooking.

This dish could be made much later in your shopping cycle using the following ingredients from the freezer: chicken, bacon, peas, corn, onion and dried porcini mushrooms.

OPTION 2: SOUP FOR PEOPLE WHO DON'T LIKE SOUP

If I have soup for my evening meal it has to be substantial enough that I'm not left looking for more food, especially high-calorie snacks. Snacking on biscuits or other treats late at night is an easy way to gain weight. Just getting one course on the table is hard enough, so I won't make soup as a first course – it has to be a complete meal.

Although this dish is served in a bowl with a spoon, there is so little liquid it's barely a soup. Think of it more like a bowl of meat, vegetables, beans and grains in a tasty broth. Serve it with fresh bread and butter and you'll be satisfied. If you put the soup and the breadmaker on in the morning, there is no preparation required in the evening.

This soup can also be made in the slow-cooker. It freezes well and can also be taken to work or school in a 'keep-warm' insulated container.

Step 1: Fry your favourite spicy sausage in a pan with oil on a medium to medium-high heat, or cook on the grill or barbecue. I like to cook fresh sausages within 1-2 days of buying them. You can cook them and keep them in the fridge for another couple of days before making the soup. Chorizo is a great choice; it's full of flavour and firm enough to slice into pieces before frying. You get delicious, crispy browned edges and the pieces will still stay together when added to the soup. Chorizo is cured and will usually last a couple of weeks in the fridge if vacuum packed. It can also be frozen. Alternatively, you can use your favourite fresh sausages. They will usually have to be cooked whole and then sliced. The pieces may fall apart when added to the soup, which doesn't matter. To minimise washing-up, I fry the sausages in the same saucepan I make the soup in.

Step 2: Remove the sausage from the pan, turn the heat down, add more oil if needed and some butter, then fry chopped onion and garlic. Depending on how spicy you like your food and how spicy your sausages are, you can also add chopped chilli, chilli paste or chilli oil. You can also add diced carrot and celery.

Step 3: Add your grain and stock. Pearl barley is a great grain to use in soups. Unlike pasta, it holds together and is harder to overcook. For two litres of chicken stock, I would add one and a half cups of rinsed pearl barley. Follow the packet instructions for the cooking time. It will usually require simmering for about 40 minutes. During this time, you can add the next few ingredients in stages. To avoid overcooking the vegetables, they can be added in the last 10 minutes of cooking.

Step 4: Add whatever other vegetables you have available, including green beans, peas, corn, mushrooms, cabbage and capsicum. You can also add fresh or dried chopped celery leaves. Bay leaves, peppercorns, parsley and fresh or dried thyme and oregano twigs can be added whole and removed at the end. Experiment with the ingredients you like.

I like to add tomatoes to the base liquid. These can be in the form of chopped fresh tomatoes, tinned tomatoes, passata, tomato paste and any combination of these. If you're using shop-bought stock and tinned tomatoes or tomato paste, you probably won't need to add any extra salt.

Lastly, I add 1-2 tins of cannellini, borlotti or red kidney beans, or chickpeas.

PASTA RAGU

The principles here are very similar to the Bolognese sauce, which is essentially a ragu. But for a beef ragu, I like to use gravy beef. Other choices are chuck or blade steak. These are more affordable cuts of beef. Talk to your butcher about other cheap cuts. These cuts do well in the slow-cooker, but if you don't have one you can just cook it on very low heat on the stove or in the oven, but you'll need to add more liquid, as explained below. The fat helps to keep the meat tender and prevents it from drying out and the tough collagen is cooked out, leaving tender meat that falls apart. You can serve this with pasta or alternatives such as rice or polenta. Sunday is often my cooking day. I might start this on a Sunday morning, first thing, before breakfast, making enough for three meals, and freeze all of it to use for midweek dinners. Then I'll put the breadmaker on, cook pancakes for breakfast, make biscuits for recess and still make another meal for the evening. To save space in the freezer, I make a heavy ragu with little sauce to freeze, and just add passata when I defrost it later to increase the volume.

Step 1: For the best flavour, fry the diced beef first in oil to brown the outside, in batches if needed. Transfer to the slow-cooker. I'll do the same if I'm adding diced pancetta. Deglaze the pan with verjuice, beef stock or red wine and reduce this liquid to about a half to a quarter of the original volume and add to the slow-cooker. I once opened a not-very-expensive red wine that I didn't like. I boiled the contents of the whole bottle to reduce the volume to about a quarter and added it to a ragu and it was delicious. You're not generally going to want to use a whole bottle of red wine up in your cooking, but if you ever end up with a bottle you don't want to drink…

Step 2: Add your other ingredients to the slow-cooker. Use minimal liquid. Not only does the slow-cooker allow you to get on with other jobs while you leave it on for 8 hours, the long cooking time means you only need to roughly chop the other ingredients. I might cut a peeled onion only into half or quarters, add garlic cloves whole and cut the carrot and celery into one-inch pieces. I might add some tomato paste, a small amount of passata and a couple of homemade frozen veal stock cubes. A cup of liquid is enough. Lay whole stems of rosemary, thyme or oregano and parsley on top of a couple of bay leaves, cover and cook on a low setting for 8 hours.

Step 3: At the end, remove the bay leaves and stems and break up the meat with a fork. To serve, toss the ragu through just-cooked pasta so the pasta is coated with the rich flavours. Penne pasta works well. The ragu freezes well and can be heated in the microwave while you cook the pasta.

If I'm not using the slow-cooker, I will use a heavy-based saucepan and start by browning the onion and garlic, which are chopped into smaller pieces. Then add and brown the pancetta and then the beef. This is a compromise if I am in a rush and can't be bothered browning the meat first, removing from the pan and adding back later. If you want to take a short cut and just add everything consecutively, you'll need to use an extra-large pot. Then add diced carrot and celery and fry before adding the liquid. Deglaze the pan and reduce the liquid. Add more passata than with the slow-cooker and about 500ml of beef stock and the herbs. Simmer on a low heat for 2-4 hours until the meat is falling apart, adding more stock if needed along the way.

Tasting along the way is important and allows you to add salt and pepper to your taste at the end of cooking. Sometimes I won't add any salt, depending on the amount of salt in the stock and passata I have used and the salt from the pancetta. If you add too much salt, you can balance it by adding a spoonful of brown sugar.

WHOLE-BAKED CAULIFLOWER

Cauliflower is not very filling but you can serve it with meat from the barbecue or top it with crispy bacon and some breadcrumbs that have been fried in butter and chopped garlic to make it more substantial.

I love it because it is so easy. When I am shopping and I see a whole cauliflower, I'm often tempted to add it to my basket as an unscheduled meal – something I don't do very often. I can't resist the idea that I don't even need to cut it up. Just remove the outer leaves, wash, dry and place whole on a baking tray. The simplest version would be to brush with olive oil and sprinkle with salt and pepper.

However, due to its mild taste, cauliflower allows you to be creative. Try covering it with your favourite spice mix. Make a paste using some oil, curry powder and some of the leftover spice mixes in your pantry.

Bake for approximately 40 minutes in a 200-degree Celsius oven or until the base is soft when tested with a skewer.

DAY 6, 7 & 8
FRIED RICE

As I get to the second week, my planning pays off. Fried rice can be made using some fresh, long-lasting ingredients like carrots and eggs, some frozen ingredients like peas and corn and some pantry items. I have included a version that can be made using just long-life ingredients and I have made this in week three.

Fried rice is a great one-dish meal that can be made from several different ingredients in large quantities. The key is in the preparation. I make sure I have everything laid out in small bowls, ready to add to the wok.

The ingredients are all cut small so there are no large chunks in the rice and the appearance is more consistent. Slices of sausage or diced meat are usually larger pieces, but still small enough to comfortably eat with a fork.

The rice: I usually steam the rice first. I have found a microwave rice cooker very quick and easy, especially for smaller volumes. I use a rice cooker when I have larger quantities. One cup of rice will be enough for two people as it will yield at least 2 cups of rice when cooked, before adding all the other ingredients.

I think the best microwave rice cookers are the ones with two lids so there is less water boiling over the top and less mess in the microwave.

I find basmati rice works well and holds together better than jasmine rice. The rice can be cooked ahead of time and stored in the fridge and it's actually better for making fried rice once it has dried out a bit. Alternatively, you can cook the rice and then, while you are getting the other ingredients ready, open the lid and fluff up the rice to let out the steam and allow it to dry out a bit.

Step 1: There are some ingredients I will cook first and then set aside in a bowl, ready to add back later. First, I might dry-roast some peanuts in a wok, with no oil, on low heat. Stir continuously as nuts will burn quickly. Remove them as soon as they start to brown and smell aromatic. I use salt-free nuts that are already roasted. Dry-roasting them again just brings out more flavour and freshness.

Step 2: Next, I might fry some sliced lap cheong sausage, a dried Chinese pork sausage with a long shelf life. Once I open a packet, I will store it in the fridge or freezer. It can also be sliced from frozen and added straight to the wok. It adds a great sweet-salty flavour to the fried rice. I don't add oil to the wok as enough oil comes out of the sausages during cooking.

Step 3: There is often even enough oil from the sausages to be able to cook the omelette. Beat 2-4 eggs and fry in the wok. Tilt the wok so the egg spreads halfway up the sides. Once the egg is set enough to turn, flip it over to cook the other side, remove from the wok, drizzle with a small amount of sesame oil and slice into thin strips.

Step 4: I will usually need to add some oil to the wok before frying the meat. I use an oil with a high smoke point (see Stir-fry, page 35). You can use chicken or beef. Chicken should be well-cooked. If you're using frozen chicken, defrost it in the fridge overnight. Beef can be sliced thinly while frozen and even cooked from frozen in a hot wok. Sear the meat and then remove.

Step 5: From now on, the ingredients are added quickly and it won't take long to finish the dish. The heat may need adjusting. Onion and garlic can burn quickly, so I often turn down the heat and add more oil if necessary before frying onion, garlic, ginger and chillies or chilli paste. Next, I add diced carrot, chopped long green beans, diced zucchini, chopped capsicum or whatever vegetables I have available. The quantities do not matter. If I have a small portion of leftover broccoli, I just chop it finely and add it. The vegetables don't need to be cooked for too long. Frozen peas and corn work well as they are the perfect size for fried rice and can be added to the wok frozen.

Step 6: Add back any meat to heat through, then add the rice, breaking up any clumps. I then add sauces before finishing with the omelette and nuts.

If I have fresh coriander to use up, I will add this before serving.

Sauces: An easy option is equal quantities of sweet chilli and dark soy sauce. Don't overdo it. I add just enough to be able to mix through evenly without any sauce sitting in the bottom of the wok. You could also just add soy sauce or, for a sweeter variation, which might please the kids, add kecap manis, a sweetened soy sauce. If you don't have any, you can use standard soy sauce with some brown sugar.

Fried rice is easy to make in large quantities, but I don't like to freeze it. It will keep in the fridge and can be heated in the microwave for a speedy second-night dinner.

You can also do a vegetarian option and try adding sliced tinned water chestnuts.

SPAGHETTI CARBONARA

Spaghetti carbonara is a great dish to master; it's tasty and affordable and uses only a few key ingredients. It's one of my favourite meals, yet I rarely order it when dining out as I don't like cream in my carbonara sauce.

There is no cream in my pasta carbonara. This can easily be made much later in the shopping cycle, depending on how long the eggs you buy will last. Use dried pasta, eggs, frozen bacon and parmesan. Use fresh parsley if available, ideally home-grown. This dish does not freeze and should be eaten fresh.

The concept is to make a mix of raw beaten egg, grated parmesan, salt and pepper. Then add the just-cooked, hot pasta and warm, cooked bacon. These ingredients then melt the cheese and gently partly cook the egg, making a creamy sauce. If the ingredients are too hot when combined, they will scramble the egg, resulting in a lumpy rather than creamy, shiny appearance.

Step 1: The first thing I do is start boiling salted water for the pasta while I get the remaining ingredients out on the bench, as it can take a while to bring to the pot to a rapid boil. If the water boils before you are ready to start cooking the pasta, you can turn it off and then it won't take long to bring back to the boil when you are ready. When cooking pasta, you want to make sure you have enough water and salt – I use about two teaspoons of salt in a pot of water. I like to use a pasta saucepan which has a colander inside the saucepan. When the pasta is cooked, the inner colander is removed to drain the pasta.

Step 2: While the water for the pasta is coming to the boil, start heating the pan to fry the bacon. While the pan is heating up, chop garlic, onion or shallots and bacon. Sometimes I make this without garlic or onion. I like to use short-back bacon as there is less fat. Bacon chops work well diced and are cheaper. As I usually have bacon in the freezer and parmesan and eggs in the fridge, this is one of my go-to meals when we start to run out of other ingredients.

Step 3: Once the frypan is warmed over medium heat, add a small amount of olive oil, even less if you're using a non-stick pan. Fry the bacon to your liking. The easiest way to avoid burning the garlic and onion may be to fry the bacon first to your liking, remove, then fry the onion or shallots and garlic and add back the bacon. I like my bacon quite crispy, so I will usually add this to the pan first and then add the onion, then garlic or shallots. (I find if I add these to the pan before the bacon, they end up burnt). Add a splash of verjuice or white wine to deglaze the pan. Turn off the heat when cooked.

Step 4: While the bacon is cooking, beat three eggs per two people, add lots of grated parmesan, sea salt, cracked pepper and chopped fresh parsley if available.

Add your pasta to the boiling water and cook until firm to the bite. There should be no crunch but it shouldn't be too soft. When the pasta is almost cooked, reheat the bacon if needed. Don't overheat.

Step 5: When the pasta is cooked, drain it and add the hot pasta to the egg mixture and mix through. The key here is to combine the ingredients quickly to disperse the heat as evenly as possible to avoid part of the sauce scrambling. Add the warm bacon mixture and mix through. Let the heat of the ingredients gently cook the egg mixture for a minute and then serve.

PORK PATTIES

Although I wouldn't keep mince for very long in the fridge, this works well for a week two meal because after my shop I make the patties quickly and freeze them, uncooked, and defrost in the fridge overnight in week two. They make a good quick weeknight dinner, pan-fried and served with steamed rice.

Step 1: Place the pork mince in a bowl and add finely chopped ingredients. Choose from the following to suit your tastes: onion, garlic, spring onion, chilli, lemongrass (white part only), kaffir lime leaves, lemon or lime zest, fresh coriander. For 500g of mince I add one beaten egg. Shape into balls with your hands, flatten into patties and freeze between layers of freezer wrap (if you're not cooking them straight away). If cooking without freezing, chilling them in the fridge for 30 minutes prior to cooking will help them retain their shape.

Step 2: Defrost the patties before pan-frying. While the patties are defrosting, prepare the sauce, so it is ready to add to the pan after the patties are cooked. Combine chicken stock, soy sauce and brown or palm sugar in ratios 3:2:1 respectively, depending on the volume of sauce you want to make. Once you have tasted this, you will probably make more sauce next time as it is delicious poured over the patties on a bed of steamed rice.

Step 3: Heat a non-stick frying pan on medium to high heat and add some oil with a high smoke point. When the oil is hot enough, fry the patties so they form a nice brown crust on each side. Then add the sauce to the pan. Let it boil and thicken. It makes a sticky sauce, which is why I use a non-stick pan.

DAY 9 & 10
SAUSAGE PASTA & OTHER 'PANTRY' PASTA

Chorizo sausages have a long shelf life and are full of flavour. Frying a couple of sliced sausages, with or without chopped onion and garlic (fresh or frozen), is one of the simplest pasta sauces. Onion and garlic will often store for at least two weeks if sourced fresh. Add extra chilli if you like it hot and frozen peas and corn.

Add some tomato passata and some tomato paste to intensify the tomato favour. You can also use tinned tomatoes instead of, or in addition to, passata. Don't overcook your pasta. When it still has some bite, drain and add to the pan with the sauce and combine well to coat the pasta with the sauce. If you don't have chorizo, you can also use salami or tinned, drained tuna.

Once you build your confidence, vary your ingredients in a tomato-based sauce. Try using chicken or beef from the freezer, defrosted in the fridge overnight. Other pantry ingredients that work well in pasta include olives, anchovies or capers.

Don't be afraid to experiment with adding herbs like thyme, oregano, basil, rosemary and parsley. These are available dried but they are easy to grow in summer.

Another delicious pasta for a light meal is to just pan-fry chopped chilli and garlic in oil and melted butter. Add just-cooked pasta, mix through and serve immediately. It doesn't have great nutritional value, but as an occasional treat, it is delicious.

If fresh basil is in season, you can make pesto and freeze it to enjoy your basil at a later time.

Pesto: Remove the leaves from a bunch of basil, wash and dry. Place in a food processor with peeled, roughly chopped garlic, salt, pepper, pine nuts, finely grated parmesan and olive oil, then blend. You need enough olive oil for the ingredients to form a paste. The pesto can be frozen in ice cube trays or even zip-lock bags. For an instant meal, just defrost and add to hot pasta. Frozen peas, heated, make a great addition.

SLOW-COOKER MEAT DISHES

I love that you can 'set and forget' with a slow-cooker. On a Sunday morning, after making pancakes and putting the breadmaker on, I often set up the slow-cooker as well as baking for the coming week's school lunch box. I do all this in about an hour, then sit down to read the paper with coffee. The house smells amazing all day.

The cheaper cuts of meat work best in a slow-cooker and the result is outstanding value for money. These dishes freeze well and make great reheated weeknight meals if I get home from work late, exhausted or both.

I prefer to fry the meat first to sear the outside for flavour. I use an enormous pot to fry 1kg of gravy beef or *osso buco* to avoid having to cook it in batches. To sear a lamb or pork shoulder, I put in a hot, hooded barbecue until the outer surface has changed colour and sealed.

Virtually no liquid needs to be added with a slow-cooker. I usually use the low setting and cook for 8 hours. Everything can be chopped roughly in large pieces, which saves on preparation time.

Lamb shoulder: Try a lamb shoulder with a few whole peeled garlic cloves, fresh rosemary and some lemon wedges. Yes, it is that simple. No need to add any liquid, there will be enough juices that come out of the meat.

Pork shoulder: For a spicy mix, add garlic and chilli or chilli powder. If you like tomatoes, add fresh tomatoes, tomato paste or passata.

For a dryer dish, just add a teaspoon each of ground coriander, ground cumin, sweet or smoky paprika and chilli powder.

You don't need to add any liquid; there will be enough liquid coming out of the meat. You'll be surprised. Add salt and pepper to your taste. For a milder pork dish, add apple, quartered and cored, and equal quantities of lemon juice and brown sugar.

When slow-cooking, using pork or lamb shoulder on the bone adds more flavour. The cooked meat will just fall off the bone when pulled with a fork. Leftover meat can be used in a pasta sauce or frozen and added to tortillas and sandwiches for lunch.

Slow-cooker curry: For a beef curry in the slow-cooker, I make a drier curry than when cooked on the stove (see Curries page 94). First, sear diced gravy beef (See Pasta ragu, Day 3-4, page 76). If I'm buying the meat as part of my fortnightly shop, I often cook the meat on the first weekend and freeze the curry for dinners in the second week, rather than keeping the meat in the fridge for over a week. But you can ask your butcher about recommended storage times. Some will vacuum pack the meat for you to lengthen storage times. Once seared, transfer the beef to the slow-cooker and add an onion, peeled and quartered, whole peeled garlic cloves, a cinnamon stick, a couple of cloves, a few chopped tomatoes and ginger. Add a teaspoonful of ground coriander and cumin, half a teaspoon of chilli powder and turmeric (or more if you like it really spicy), some curry leaves and cook on low for 8 hours.

DAYS 11, 12, 13 & 14
CHICKPEA FRITTERS

These are great to make using long-shelf-life ingredients in week two. They are a vegetarian meal option and can be served with a salad, freshly baked bread and yoghurt dipping sauce. They are also useful as a light lunch and for school lunch boxes and are affordable to make.

Falafels are traditionally deep-fried balls. I usually shallow-fry mine in a pan, to use less oil. I, therefore, make a flatter patty to make sure they are heated through as they cook at a lower temperature than with deep-frying. These are an extension of the traditional falafel and you can add various spices and ingredients to suit your taste. By keeping a can of chickpeas in the pantry and breadcrumbs in the freezer, this budget meal is always on hand.

Fritter mix: The basis of these fritters is a can of rinsed chickpeas, mashed or pulsed in a food processor or blender. If you have more time you can also use dried chickpeas, soaked in water overnight, then boiled in fresh water for an hour before draining. To help bind the patty, add an egg and some breadcrumbs for a lighter texture. Homemade breadcrumbs, made from leftover bread and kept in the freezer, can be added to the food processor still frozen. This will give you the consistency to roll the fritters into balls. If the mixture is too wet, the patties will fall apart. You can add a small amount of lemon juice and mix as you go to make sure the mixture doesn't become too wet. If it does, just add more breadcrumbs. Ingredients you can choose from for flavouring include: lemon zest, finely chopped shallots, fried onion, fresh parsley or dried parsley, finely grated parmesan, ground cumin, ground coriander, ground turmeric, curry powder, chilli powder or chopped chilli, sea salt and ground black pepper. Experiment with different flavours and amounts. Try something different every time. When pulsed in the food processor, this will make a paste that you can roll into balls and then flatten to make patties.

Another option is to coat them in breadcrumbs before frying. I like to use panko breadcrumbs mixed with lemon zest, grated parmesan, sea salt and pepper.

Refrigerating the patties before cooking helps them keep together when cooking. This is an ideal quick recipe to prepare in the morning, ready to fry for a quick evening meal.

Dipping sauce: A simple dipping sauce is some Greek yoghurt with finely chopped garlic. Add enough lemon juice to get the consistency you want and season with salt. Both garlic and lemon can be kept in the freezer and most Greek yoghurt keeps in the fridge for a couple of weeks.

Lemon-chicken RISOTTO

Although I have already described how to make risotto, this highlights how a risotto can be made from freezer ingredients a week after your last shop. The ingredients from the freezer include:

- Diced chicken thigh fillets, frozen in vacuum pack. These are best defrosted in the fridge for 24 hours before using.
- Garlic.
- Chopped raw onions. These can be kept in the freezer in zip-lock bags.

- I like adding caramelised leeks to this dish. Because the leeks won't stay fresh for that long, I will caramelise them soon after purchasing and freeze them to use later. It is more economical to buy a whole bunch of leeks or bag of onions and caramelise them to freeze in portions. Once cooled, muffin cups are a good portion size for freezing.
- Homemade chicken stock.
- Fresh, frozen chillies.
- Whole lemons can be frozen but should last a couple of weeks in the fridge. Both zest and juice can be added to the risotto.
- Frozen peas and corn.

Other pantry items include Arborio or Carnaroli rice, oil, butter, grated parmesan, salt and ground black pepper.

SAGE BUTTER GNOCCHI

Gnocchi can be bought fresh, frozen and now even ready to pan-fry with no boiling required. Sage is very easy to grow and can be harvested all year round in Australia. Melt butter until foaming. Add washed and well-dried sage leaves (I dry them with absorbent paper) and fry until crisp. Transfer to absorbent paper to drain the butter. Add cooked gnocchi to the pan with sea salt and pepper and fry until partly browned. (Note: if your gnocchi require cooking first in boiling water, make sure you have a rapid boil and only cook them briefly. Take them off the heat as soon as they start to rise to the surface. They are so easy to overcook, which results in a mushy mess, so I prefer the type you can just add to the frypan without boiling in water.) Add back the sage leaves to heat through and serve. For a more substantial meal, you can add pre-roasted pumpkin pieces and toasted pine nuts. A whole pumpkin will keep for weeks.

CURRIES

I will start with vegetable curry as it's probably the easiest curry to make and it proves you can still have vegetables two weeks after you've shopped. Vegetables such as potatoes, pumpkin and carrot will easily keep for two weeks in the fridge, possibly longer if you buy good-quality fresh ingredients.

Try to find a good curry powder from an Asian food shop. These are often inexpensive and sold in larger amounts like 500g bags and are superior to the curry powder from supermarkets. Asian stores are usually also a good source for savings on spices. Ask the staff to recommend curry powders, one for vegetables and one for meat. If you think a vegetable curry won't be substantial enough for your evening meal, add cashews, hard-boiled eggs and tofu and serve with brown rice. Curries freeze well.

Vegetable curry

Step 1: In a heavy-based pan, fry spices such as cumin seeds, fennel seeds, fenugreek seeds and a generous amount of curry leaves (about 20 leaves) in oil or ghee, with or without chopped onion. You can use fresh or dried curry leaves. If they're still attached to the stem they can be added whole. Just remove the stem before serving. The leaves will usually fall off during cooking. Then add the curry powder. Follow the instructions on the curry powder regarding recommended quantities, which may be a couple of tablespoons.

Step 2: Once you have fried the curry powder and spices until they are aromatic, you can add water and vegetable or chicken stock. Bring to a simmer, then add the vegetables in order of cooking times. Cooking time will vary depending on the size of the pieces you have cut and the quantity. Fifteen minutes may be all that is required. As the curry powder has a lot of flavour, it is fine to just add water instead of stock. I like to cut the vegetables into bite-size pieces so the dish can be comfortably eaten with a fork. These smaller pieces will also cook faster. You want to cook the vegetables until tender but not until they are breaking up and falling apart. Add the vegetables that require the longest cooking time first. These vegetables can be stored in the fridge for two weeks and could be added in the following order: potatoes, pumpkin, carrot and cauliflower. You can also add frozen peas, fried or marinated tofu and hard-boiled eggs, peeled and halved. If you are making this dish in the first week after shopping, you can add vegetables like green beans and cabbage. A vegetable curry is a great way to use up your leftover vegetables. Add roasted, unsalted cashews before serving with brown rice.

Meat and chicken curry: If you're making a beef or other meat curry, choose a curry powder suited to your meat-based curry. You can ask an Asian spice shop for a recommendation. For a chicken curry, try frying the following spices before adding your curry powder: one cinnamon stick, a couple of star anise, half a dozen cloves, a teaspoon each of cumin and fennel seeds and 20 curry leaves. The smell alone will be worth it. The meat or chicken can be fried first to seal, removed from the pan and added back later, or added after frying the spices, before adding the stock. In many Asian recipes you add the water first, then the stock, and then just add the raw meat to the boiling liquid. Although it's not the method I learnt, it seems to give a satisfactory result and is much less hassle. Though I think you get more flavour from browning the meat first. Meat can be stored in the freezer. If sliced frozen, it can even be added frozen straight to the boiling stock.

BONUS DISH: ROAST CHICKEN

I think it might be because I have an English mother, but I believe if there is one dish you need to master to impress others, that has broad appeal, it's roast chicken. It's good for special occasion celebrations as well as weekend dinners. If you practise making it regularly it will become effortless and take the stress out of entertaining.

In Australia, even a free-range chicken is not that expensive. A good-quality free-range chicken will give the best flavour. I have been surprised by the quality of a free-range chicken from my local discount supermarket for under A$10.

Preparation: The chicken will cook faster if you take it out of the fridge half an hour before cooking, but it shouldn't be left out for two hours and there is no need to wash it. If it has been sitting in juices, pat it dry with some good-quality paper towel that won't disintegrate when drying. Remember to wash your hands well before and after handling raw chicken and anything else that has come into contact with it. Most chicken is covered in bacteria that is killed when cooked. It's essential to make sure you don't transfer the bacteria to other food, surfaces or utensils before you cook the chicken. Never place your cooked chicken back on the same chopping board you had the raw chicken on as you will transfer the bacteria back onto it.

If you've never roasted a chicken, first make sure you know which way is up! The large cavity is at the tail end and the bird is roasted breast side up. The breast will be the thicker meat either side of the midline compared to the bony back. Placing some lemon wedges and herbs in the large cavity will add flavour. I like to use up whatever I have around. It might be half a leftover lemon in the fridge, the tops of some spring onion or onion wedges, celery tops and celery leaves and a selection of herbs from the garden: thyme, sage and bay leaves.

Herb butter: Next, I make a herb butter with salted butter, chopped garlic, fresh parsley and sea salt. I rub this over the top of the chicken (breast and legs). I also lift the skin off the breast by pushing my finger along the breast meat under the edge of the skin and push some herb butter under the skin. If you tie the end of the legs together with some string, this will keep everything in the cavity. Tucking the wing tips under the bird will prevent them from burning. I also place a small amount of oil or duck fat in the baking pan and drizzle or smear some over any parts of the chicken not covered with the herb butter. Choose a baking pan you can place on the stovetop later to make the gravy.

Cooking: I prefer to cook the chicken in my hooded four-gas-burner barbecue. It may be harder to regulate the temperature compared with a conventional oven but I don't usually find the temperature needs to be that exact – about 200-220 degrees Celsius.

I often heat the barbecue to a much higher temperature and then turn down the heat when I put the chicken in. I heat the barbecue with all four burners on full. When I put the chicken in, I turn the middle two burners down to very low and have the outer two on about half their maximum setting.

I find basting easier in the barbecue as I just lift the hood rather than lifting the chicken in and out of the oven. About every 20 minutes, use a baster or spoon to collect some of the juices in the pan and pour these over the skin to moisten and aid browning.

The best way to ensure the chicken is cooked is to use a meat thermometer. I cook to 85 degrees Celsius and make sure the thermometer is in the thick part of the thigh, not touching the bone, as this red meat takes the longest to cook. When I think it's done I'll often test by moving the thermometer around to several places to make sure the bird is fully cooked. Wrap in foil to rest while you prepare the gravy.

Gravy: To make the gravy, you separate some of the fat from the juices. If you tip the roasting pan, the fat will sit in a layer above the juices and you can remove it with a spoon or baster and discard. Add a spoonful of flour to the juices left in the pan and place on the stovetop. Once browned, whisk in some hot chicken stock. You can also add a spoonful of red currant jelly. This will add some sweetness and flavour and balance any acidity if you've used lemon or added wine to the gravy. You can deglaze the pan with red or white wine or verjuice, but the flavour is great with just stock. Add sea salt and ground black pepper to taste. Tasting the gravy is important. I have never been a great gravy maker but with practice, I have improved.

Carving: While you make the gravy, the chicken has time to rest before you carve it. Resting the chicken before you carve it keeps the meat moist by retaining more juices. If you cut the chicken straight away, more juices will run out, losing flavour and resulting in drier meat.

Many people are afraid of carving the chicken, but not me! As a surgeon, I am pretty confident in this department. If you have never carved a chicken, like anything, practice is the key. To start, cut through the joint where the thighbone connects to the carcass to remove the leg together with the thigh fillet. (If you just pull firmly, both the wings and the thighs will come away, but removing them with a carving knife and fork will impress your diners.) Then cut through the joint to separate the thigh fillet from the drumstick.

Next you can cut the breast off in one big piece with the wing attached, to remove later. Slide the knife down the midline alongside the breastbone, following the bone. You don't need much force and you don't need to cut through any bone. You cut between the breast meat and the ribcage. As you follow the bone, you will cut downwards toward the bench and then start to head out to the side to finish removing the breast. You can then place the breast on the board and slice it to serve. Alternatively, you can carve the breast in slices from the roast rather than removing it one large piece, which looks fancier when carving at the table. To slice, you cut each slice obliquely from the outer surface, starting with the knife near the midline and cutting on an angle sideways to slice off a piece of breast meat.

The wings have three sections: a pointy tip, a middle section and the third, widest part called the drumette, where it connects to the ribcage. You want to cut through the joint between the third part of the wing and the ribcage and not cut through the bone. Pulling on the wing opens up the joint and makes it easier to get to. You can cut through the joint with a carving knife or poultry scissors.

Sides

What are you going to serve with your roast chicken? Just about anything will do, from salad to roast vegetables. A salad is less stressful and is therefore a good place to start. After you become more confident, you can prepare your side dishes while the chicken is roasting. Vegetables can be glazed in a small amount of butter and water easily in one frypan (see page 59).

Roast vegetables: Roasting vegetables is easy and, together with roast chicken, makes a great winter meal.

I take the vegetables out of the fridge with the chicken. I usually make potatoes and carrots and a third vegetable such as pumpkin, parsnip or sweet potato. I put a pot of water on to boil while I prepare the chicken and peel and quarter the potatoes. As soon as the water is boiling, I place the potatoes in to parboil. The potatoes are parboiled when they are soft but still firm when you pass a skewer through them. I boil them in my pasta saucepan so I can just lift out the inner colander section when they are done and shake them to fluff up the outer surfaces. Then I place them in a baking tray with duck fat. Duck fat makes great roast potatoes and carrots and it's worth investing in a jar. You only need a small amount as, once melted, a little goes a long way. It only needs to be enough to coat the vegetables, not a thick layer at the bottom. Duck fat has a high smoke point and it is unlikely to go rancid. (You can usually tell if oil is rancid by smelling it.) After cooking, just strain the duck fat and it can be re-used. Store it in the fridge or freezer.

I used to roast the vegetables in the hooded barbecue with the chicken but I found the vegetables would burn if they were sitting alongside the chicken in the centre. It's much easier to roast the vegetables in the oven. If you don't have a barbecue, you can roast the chicken and vegetables in the oven. If you're placing the vegetables in the same roasting pan as the chicken, put duck fat in the base of the pan. Some people add stock to the roasting pan, but I find I then don't get crispy chicken and vegetables, so I only add the stock to the pan when I make the gravy.

You can also cook the vegetables in the same oven, with the chicken, in different pans. If you're cooking different vegetables in one pan, you might add them at different times or remove some early and set aside. Depending on the size of your oven, you may not have room for the chicken and separate pans for each vegetable. This is another advantage of cooking the chicken on the barbecue. I still sometimes combine my vegetable in one pan, just to save on washing-up. This is how I discovered my other vegetables were also better roasted in duck fat. Finally, I was able to get my roast carrots close to the delicious, sweet memories I have of how my grandmother made them.

If you cut the carrots too small, they dry out. They do need to cook for a long time, but this will depend on the size of the pieces. I generally cut them in half midway. I then cut the lower, more tapered section in half lengthways and the thicker, top section into quarters lengthways. With the potatoes parboiled, both the carrots and potatoes will take about an hour to roast. (When peeling the carrots, save the peel and tops to use for stock.)

Top this meal off with fresh, warm bread, which you can set to come out of your breadmaker an hour before your meal is ready. Serve it with butter and you have a feast fit for a king or queen!

One roast chicken will usually feed four adults. If you need to feed up to eight, then you can do two chickens on the barbecue and put the vegetables in your oven.

Don't disregard a roast chicken dinner if you're cooking for one or two people. A roast dinner is a great way to treat yourself. When cooking for two people, after dinner, I remove all of the leftover chicken meat. This can be frozen, although I usually plan to use it the next night in a meal like a risotto, casserole or curry. It can also be used to prepare sandwich fillings as described in the lunch section.

Chicken stock

Don't throw out the carcass. I use a lot of chicken stock for risotto, gravy, curries, casseroles and soups; up to a couple of litres a week. Homemade stock is superior and buying good-quality chicken stock is not cheap. By using homemade stock, I can save around A$20 per shop or more. You don't have to make the stock straight after the roast dinner. If I plan a roast dinner on a Friday or Saturday night, I eat the leftover chicken for dinner the next night and make the chicken stock the next day.

Step 1: I place the chicken carcass, with small amounts of meat left on it, into my pasta saucepan in the fridge. The next day, I boil it for 4-6 hours. You can add your other ingredients at the same time but then you will add less water so you won't get as much stock. I fill the pan with as much water as I can to cover the chicken, but leave enough room at the top so it doesn't boil over when simmering. Keep the lid on to retain as much liquid as possible. It will also reach boiling point much faster with the lid on. Once boiling, reduce the heat to a simmer for 4 hours.

Step 2: Remove the chicken carcass. I use the pasta saucepan because I can simply lift out the inner colander to remove the carcass. Add your other ingredients and boil for another hour. The other ingredients include: celery and leek tops, carrot, onion and garlic, though there may be enough garlic flavour from the garlic butter used to roast the chicken. I add any remaining vegetable pieces in the fridge that I want to use up such as mushroom, spring onion and tomato. You can also add parmesan rind, a few black peppercorns, lemon peel or zest, bay leaves and any leftover herbs such as parsley or thyme. However, as there are still herbs in the cavity of the carcass, I usually find there is enough flavour that you don't need to add more.

Step 3: After boiling for an hour, remove the big pieces and strain with a fine sieve.

If finding time to allow the stock to simmer for several hours is difficult, you can let it simmer in a slow-cooker for 8 hours or do it in stages. I have even taken it off the simmer and allowed it to cool enough to transfer to the fridge, before putting it back on to boil later. Or I have turned the stove off, left the house for a short errand, come home and turned it on again. Cooking the bones for long periods releases the collagen protein to form gelatin, which adds flavour and has nutritional benefits.

You can also buy uncooked chicken bones from your butcher, usually at a low cost, to give your stock even more flavour. Cook for up to 12 hours.

Step 4: I then transfer to 500ml containers and cool in the fridge, which allows the fat to settle and solidify on the top. Remove this and discard before transferring the containers to the freezer if you are not using it in the next three days.

PART THREE

BAKING & DESSERTS

Educate a woman to cook and you educate a family to cook.

Baking is traditionally an area where you are meant to follow a recipe but I challenge you to make your own recipes. Follow my basic method, then be creative and experiment with different ingredients and amounts.

BISCUITS

A basic biscuit recipe is a staple. I usually make at least one batch of biscuits a week for school recess. They are so quick and easy that even if we feel like some biscuits on a weeknight, I just make a batch. I use an electric mixer – a worthwhile investment, especially for baking. I prefer knowing the biscuits I am eating are made with all-natural ingredients. If I am watching Netflix with my son, I would rather get off the sofa and make biscuits for us than just keep sitting on the sofa, eating biscuits from a packet.

There are so many biscuit recipes out there that if you don't or have never made biscuits, don't let not having a recipe stop you. Be creative, experiment with a few different ingredients and amounts. Chances are your failures will still be good enough to eat. Children love eating the raw dough and it's lovely when the kitchen smells of freshly baked biscuits.

Ingredient proportions: Try the following proportions: 100g sugar, 100g butter, 150g plain flour and half a teaspoon of baking powder. I use caster sugar. You can try using brown sugar or half caster sugar and half brown sugar to see what difference it makes. These proportions make about 12 biscuits, which I would call 'half a batch'. It's a good idea to stick to smaller quantities when you're starting or experimenting with new ideas and it helps with portion control. In this recipe I will vary the amount of flour, usually from 100-150g depending on the consistency of the other ingredients. I use less flour if I'm only adding dry ingredients like spices and more flour if I'm adding liquid ingredients like lemon juice. I will add the flour a spoonful at a time to the mixer while mixing until I see it is the right consistency. I stop when the mixture just starts to form large clumps, before it becomes too crumbly. This is a consistency which is easy to roll a spoonful in my hands and flatten to make biscuits. If it's too moist, it is sticky and hard to roll; if it's too dry and crumbly, you won't be able to form a ball. Once you are confident with the basic method, you will just be able to add the right amount of flour from the container without even measuring it, saving on washing-up. I never bother to sift the flour for biscuits.

Step 1: First, whisk the butter and sugar together in a mixer. It's important that the butter is at room temperature and not straight from the fridge. This means you will need to do some planning in advance. If I have not planned to bake, I slice fine slithers of butter and lay them out on a plate to allow it to reach room temperature faster or I use soft, spreadable butter in a tub. Just make sure this is a brand that is still pure butter, not margarine or a blend. It will take several minutes to whisk the butter and sugar. It will change colour to a much paler yellow and the consistency will be lighter.

Step 2: Add the flour and baking powder. I usually add it all at once without sifting to save on time and washing-up and I change the mixer attachment from the balloon whisk to the flat mixer. I just stand the mixing bowl on my scale, set it to zero and add the dry ingredients directly to the mixing bowl with the whisked butter and sugar, to save on washing-up.

Egg: It is not necessary to add an egg and if you love eating raw biscuit dough, you may prefer not to have raw egg in your mixture. Adding an egg will make the dough moist and cause the biscuits to rise and brown more when cooked. Why not try with and without an egg to see the difference? Use a small egg if you're making half a batch (12 biscuits). You can also experiment with adding just the egg white.

Flours: Experiment with your flour. If you have self-raising flour to use up, leave out the baking powder. You could also try substituting half the flour with rice flour or cornflour.

From this basic biscuit recipe there are several flavour options:

- For **plain vanilla** biscuits, just adding a teaspoon of natural vanilla essence will bring the mixture together.

- Add **choc chips** – add and mix until it looks like the number of chocolate chips you like in your biscuits. If you're not sure where to start, try mixing in 50g of chocolate chips.

- **Lemon and poppy seed**: add the zest and juice of half a lemon and 2 teaspoons of poppy seeds. The juice will make the mixture wetter, so it will be easier to make into biscuits if you refrigerate it for 1 hour beforehand.

- **Spices:** adding mixed spices is one of my favourite variations. Try combining the following spices to suit your tastes. Use equal amounts, maybe half a teaspoon for half a batch of biscuits of: ground ginger, ground nutmeg, ground cardamom. For cinnamon, I would either use the same amount or double the amount compared to the other spices (so 1 teaspoon) and for ground cloves, half the amount (so a quarter teaspoon).

- **Peanut paste** is a great substitute for butter. Try replacing half or all the butter with peanut paste or another nut paste. You can also add chopped nuts.

Step 3: Overall, you get a better result if you refrigerate the dough for an hour before baking. This reduces the chance of the dough spreading when cooking and improves the flavour. This is an advantage if you are organised and prepare the dough in advance or even the night before. You can then have biscuits in the oven within minutes. Biscuit dough also freezes well. Roll into logs and wrap in plastic wrap. Then cut off the number of biscuits you want to bake. There is no need to defrost. Once cut, they can be baked immediately and may only need a couple of extra minutes in the oven compared with room-temperature dough.

Rolling smaller biscuits and then flattening them will increase the crispness and mean there is less of a soft, chewy centre, so modify to suit your tastes.

Make sure you leave enough room between each biscuit on the tray. I will usually have 6 biscuits per baking tray and I line the tray with a sheet of baking paper to reduce washing-up.

Step 4: Bake. Baking in a fan-forced oven can help to even out oven temperatures, but it usually reduces the temperature required from 175 down to 150 degrees Celsius. Temperatures vary considerably depending on the oven, so get to know your oven well. Do you need to turn your trays around halfway because the front or back is browning faster or swap the top and bottom trays around? If your top shelf cooks faster, these may need to be removed earlier. Often, 10-12 minutes of baking is enough. Set a timer if you are likely to get distracted or forget. I can tell when the biscuits are done based on the smell. Once the strong, delicious smell is coming from the oven, they are ready. (This is before you get that burning smell). Leave the biscuits for a minute on the trays before transferring to wire racks to cool. If you try to transfer them immediately, they will be so soft they will crack or break. If you leave them on the hot trays for too long, they will continue to cook from the residual heat in the trays and the bottoms may brown or burn.

SLICES

HEALTHY SLICE

Oats are a great source of energy, fibre and antioxidants and can help with cholesterol and blood-sugar control. This basic slice can be varied to add several different ingredients.

Step 1: I place a large microwave-proof jug on the kitchen scale and add equal weighed amounts of melted butter, rolled oats, plain wholemeal flour and honey. By using this ratio of equal weight amounts you can vary the quantity you make to suit your baking pan size. I measure the butter first in a glass jug and then heat it on low in the microwave until the butter is just melted. Then I place the jug back on the scale to add the rest of the ingredients, zeroing the scale between each addition. For this type of baking, the quantities don't have to be that exact. I then add my extras. You can add as many as you like. I love this slice filled with lots of extras, so I might add double the quantity of the basic ingredients listed above so I can have more additions. For example, if I'm using 170g each of the butter, oats, flour and honey, I then add 170g of chocolate chips and 170g of chopped nuts. Other great combinations include chocolate chips and glacé cherries, or sultanas and nuts. I often add several different ingredients to use up leftover small amounts in the pantry, including dried fruit, peel or coconut. Any of the items in the Muesli recipe (see page 131) could also be added. Mix all the ingredients together well.

Step 2: Transfer the mixture to a slice tray lined with baking paper. Experiment to work out the ratio of ingredients required for your slice tray and the thickness you want for your slice. I use a 33x18 centimetre tray. Press down firmly using your hands, a spatula or even the bottom of a flat glass. I bake it in a fan-forced oven at 175 degrees Celsius for about 15 minutes, or until the smell from the oven is just right and it looks golden-brown on top. Let it cool a bit in the pan before you try to take it out otherwise it will break. Cut it while still warm with a sharp cook's knife.

I make this on a Sunday for school recess and it will keep in an airtight container until Friday – if it's not devoured sooner.

BISCUIT BASE SLICE

Another easy option for the non-baker to try is to make a base using crumbled digestive biscuits. The number of biscuits you use will depend on how thick you want the base and the size of your slice tray.

Step 1: Break the biscuits up to form a fine crumb. The finer the crumb, the better it holds together. You can crush the biscuits in a food processor but putting them in a plastic bag and crushing them with a rolling pin is great fun for kids. You bind the crumbs together with melted butter to form a mixture that you can press into the slice pan. For half a packet of biscuits (200g), you might need half the weight of melted butter (100g), preferably unsalted. Add a couple of tablespoons of caster sugar or try it without adding sugar.

Step 2: Once mixed, press the base mixture into a pan lined with baking paper and cover with toppings of your choice. Ingredients you can use include: whole or chopped nuts, peanut paste, chopped marshmallows, dried or glacé fruit, chopped fudge and chocolate chips. You should use at least one of the soft ingredients like marshmallows, fudge, chocolate chips or peanut paste, as this will melt to hold your topping and dry ingredients together.

Step 3: Bake at approximately 175 degrees Celsius (depending on your oven) for 15-20 minutes or until the soft ingredients are melted.

APPLE CRUMBLE

Apple crumble is a crowd pleaser and a great way to get fruit into your diet if you are not good at eating fruit. It can be made in one large dish or in individual ramekins. It can be frozen and baked straight from the freezer, allowing most of the preparation to be done in advance. Serve alone for a healthier option or with ice cream or cream. You can also use other fruits in your crumble or combine fruits, such as rhubarb and pear.

Step 1: Peel and slice the apples, then stew them on the stove with a couple of tablespoons of water (you don't need much) until they are soft, but not falling apart. You can add cinnamon and cloves for spice. A little sugar will reduce the fruit's tartness, but the tartness can help to balance the sweetness of the crumble topping and ice cream, so I don't usually add sugar to the apples. Lemon juice will help prevent the apples from browning while you're preparing them, especially if there are a large number of apples to peel and cut.

Step 2: Transfer the stewed apple to a buttered baking dish.

Step 3: Make the crumble. Traditionally, this is made by rubbing cold butter into flour and sugar, using your hands. You can also add some cinnamon and nutmeg. You can use the same proportions as the biscuit recipe: 100g sugar and butter and 150g flour. If you don't like getting your hands dirty, there is a way to cheat. Your topping will be more clumpy than crumbly, but it will taste just as delicious. You stir raw oats and melted butter into the flour and sugar. First, melt the butter (about 150g) in a covered jug in the microwave on low heat until just melted. Place the jug on your scale and zero it, then add 150g plain flour, 50g oats and 100g sugar with a half a teaspoon of cinnamon and stir to combine. If you're making a larger crumble, double the quantities. Another alternative is to use cold butter and blend in a food processor until a fine crumble forms.

This will be finer than crumbling by hand and the microwave method will be coarser.

Step 4: Add the crumble topping to the dish and bake at about 160 degrees Celsius for 30 minutes or until golden-brown on top and smelling delicious.

CHOCOLATE SAUCE OR GANACHE

Being able to whip up a fantastic chocolate sauce in the microwave is a skill worth perfecting. It is an instant hit with children and can be added to ice cream for an easy dessert. You can also add fruit such as banana and chopped nuts. The traditional method of gently melting the chocolate in a double boiler is less risky as you have more control. Learning to do it in the microwave is faster and saves on washing-up, but there are only seconds between the chocolate melting and seizing. But if you need more excitement in your life, or you don't have a double boiler, give it a go!

Trick 1: Use the best-quality chocolate chips you can afford. This will give a far superior result than a bottle of shop-bought 'chocolate' topping. You should preferably use dark chocolate, at least 50% cocoa. Traditionally, chocolate ganache is made with double cream, which has at least 48% fat. The higher fat content means the cream won't separate when heated. Start with equal quantities of chocolate and cream, but you can vary it to suit your tastes.

Trick 2: Don't heat the chocolate too much, otherwise it will seize and look dry, lumpy and gritty. To avoid this happening, microwave it on a lower setting, 30 seconds at a time. Remove and stir every 30 seconds. You want to stop before all the chocolate is fully melted as there will be enough residual heat in the mixture for the last bit of chocolate to continue to melt after you remove it from the microwave. Stir or whisk to bring it to a glossy, shiny mixture. If you think it is too warm, quickly add a few more chocolate chips or some cream to bring the temperature down, stirring continuously. I often don't have cream in my fridge and will substitute it with milk, even skim milk, or some vanilla ice cream. I've even made this using up leftover crème fraîche or mascarpone.

PART FOUR

BREAKFASTS

Give a man a meal and he's happy. Teach a man to cook and the whole family's happy.

Intermittent fasting has become popular for weight control and weight loss but this doesn't mean you have to miss breakfast; you can just have breakfast much later. For us, a perfect weekend is a day spent at home, relaxing in our pyjamas, and having a late breakfast. We then often skip lunch and won't eat anything until the evening meal. We love a good breakfast and can even have two breakfasts: one small, early breakfast before an exercise session for energy, like toast, and a large, cooked breakfast afterwards.

SCRAMBLED EGGS

Eggs are a wonderfully nutritious breakfast. In our house, a favourite meal is scrambled eggs served on buttered toast, using homemade bread from our breadmaker. It's also a perfect light dinner.

There are scrambled eggs and then there are scrambled eggs. You don't want hard, tough or dry, clumped scrambled eggs, or the partly cooked, runny type. After tasting these scrambled eggs, my son has never wanted the scrambled eggs from a café or hotel buffet.

The trick is to cook the eggs slowly. This just requires time and patience, but the ingredients are only eggs and butter for the pan. Choose fresh eggs, free-range, organic where possible, and real butter, not margarine.

Fresh eggs will sink to the bottom of a bowl of water and lie sideways. The more air in the egg, the less fresh they are, and they start to stand upright or not lie at the bottom of the water. If they float, they're off!

The pan: You want the right pan – one that gives a low, slow, even heat. I use a heavy-based, non-stick pan. You want to heat the pan slowly on a very low heat, so it doesn't get too hot. The pan should also not be too big. If your egg mixture is spread too thinly over the base, it is more likely to cook too quickly. The eggs should form a layer of about 1cm in the pan.

Beating the eggs: You might want to beat your eggs before you get the pan ready but it can get a bit boring waiting for the pan to heat up slowly. I often put the pan on the lowest gas setting I have to allow it time to heat evenly, while I get the eggs and butter out of the fridge and put the toast on. Crack the desired number of eggs – I usually allow three eggs per person.

Beat the eggs well with a fork or whisk until the mixture is an even consistency. I have tried adding water or milk to this mixture but I think just eggs works best, though it is a bit more effort to beat them well. My indulgence here is to add truffle salt. Although this is an expensive ingredient, the flavour it adds is fantastic and my first jar lasted five years. You only need a small amount, maybe a quarter of a teaspoon depending on your taste, how strong the flavour of the product you use is and the number of eggs you are using.

The expense will seem worth it when it turns scrambled eggs into a substitute for an evening meal and an alternative to a meat-based meal. The truffle flavour goes well with eggs but it is not something that appeals to everyone.

Cooking the eggs: When adding the butter to the pan, if it melts quickly and starts to bubble and foam straight away, the pan is too hot, so take it off the heat and wait a bit before adding the eggs.

Alternatively, you can add the butter to the pan when you turn on the heat. Once the butter has melted, and just before or as it starts to show fine bubbles, add the beaten eggs and start stirring. Adding the cool egg mixture to the pan will cool the pan down, but if the egg mixture on the bottom of the pan starts to cook straight away, remove the pan from the heat and keep stirring, allowing it to cool a bit, before returning to a lower heat. You don't want your eggs to start cooking as soon as they hit the pan.

Continuous stirring over a low heat prevents large clumps from forming where some egg mixture is cooked more than others. By cooking slowly, at a lower temperature, your mixture will thicken evenly and change to a pale yellow colour with less clumping.

The smoother the consistency, the better. You may think the egg is not cooked but you will see a definite change in colour and consistency. This method results in smoother, creamier, richer eggs.

Remember, even once the heat is turned off, the eggs will continue to cook from the heat in the pan, so once they are done you need to get them out of the pan and onto your toast as soon as possible. Once you master this you can always have a simple but spectacular meal any time of the day. If managing the heat in the pan is too difficult to master, the eggs can be cooked over boiling water in a bain-marie or double-boiler saucepan.

At the end of cooking, add salt, truffle salt, pepper or fresh herbs such as chopped chives or parsley.

PANCAKES

I've made pancakes almost every Sunday for seven years and I'm still going. I would hate to calculate just how many pancakes I have cooked but that's not nearly as frightening as thinking about the number of pancakes my son has eaten in his lifetime. Hang on, let's stop right there. I do need to calculate this. If he eats a batch of 12 pancakes a week, and I make these about 45 weeks out of the year, then, over the past 10 years, he has eaten approximately 5400 pancakes so far. I can say I am pretty well-rehearsed in this department and can make a batch of pancake batter in five minutes without thinking. These light, fluffy pancakes are worth perfecting.

Equipment: I use an electric jug blender to mix the batter and an electric stand mixer to whisk the egg whites separately.

I cook the pancakes on an electric plate as I can cook more pancakes at once than with a frying pan.

Ingredients: You will need eggs, buttermilk, plain flour, baking powder or bicarbonate of soda and butter for cooking. The proportions for the batter are: for every egg, add 100g plain flour, 165g buttermilk and a quarter to half a teaspoon of baking powder. This will make about four pancakes or one average serve.

Step 1: Turn on the pan or plate to medium heat so it heats up while you make the batter. If you use a heavy-based frying pan, this gives it time to heat evenly. Use an egg separator to separate your eggs. Place the yolks in the jug blender and the whites in the mixer bowl. Turn on the mixer to whisk the egg whites, gradually turning up the speed until they form soft peaks. While they are mixing, place the jug blender (with the egg yolks in it), on the kitchen scale and zero it. Add the buttermilk, re-zero the scale, then add the flour and baking powder and blend until thoroughly combined. Then stop immediately; don't over-mix it.

Add the whisked egg white to the batter. Gently stir it in by hand until just combined. The batter is ready. Don't use the electric blender to mix through the egg whites as this will remove the air needed to make them fluffy.

Step 2: Melt plenty of butter in the pan. The pan should be hot enough that the butter melts quite quickly and starts foaming yellow but doesn't turn brown straight away. Add enough butter to coat the pan in a thin layer, but not so much that you have a puddle of melted butter that will splash when you add your batter or turn your pancakes. You should be able to pour the batter into the pan before the butter browns. I pour the batter straight from the electric jug blender until the pancake is the size I want. It is easy to pour to the size you want because the mixture is so thick.

Make the pancakes about the size of a saucer or small side plate. If you make them too big, they will be harder to flip. It will take at least 5 minutes before they are ready to flip, especially the first lot, as your batter has just cooled the pan down. You want to wait until bubbles appear on the top of the uncooked surface. This means they should be cooked enough to flip without splashing or breaking apart. The second side won't take as long to cook. I usually add more butter to the pan when turning the pancakes as the delicious flavour of the butter when it's cooked crispy on the outside is the best part.

I often go and do various jobs while the pancakes are cooking and I can easily forget about them, so I now set a timer on my watch for 3 or 5 minutes for each side.

These pancakes freeze well and can be reheated in the microwave, for about 30 seconds each side, making an easy breakfast that even a small child can get ready themselves.

These pancakes are delicious enough to eat on their own or you can add pure maple syrup. Pure maple syrup is very expensive but look out for when it is on sale as it is a natural sweetener and you only need a small amount. It has a far superior taste to the sugary maple-flavoured syrups. Poor a small enough amount on top of the pancake, not so much that it runs off the side edges, and spread it thinly with a knife.

One bottle of pure maple syrup is probably cheaper than one serve of pancakes served with maple-flavoured syrup at a café. Note there is no sugar in this pancake batter.

Notes for absolute beginner cooks:

1. When separating eggs, make sure not to let the yolk break to avoid any yolk contaminating your egg whites. The smallest amount of yolk will stop the whites from whisking.

2. When mixing the egg whites, start the electric mixer on medium until bubbles appear, then increase the speed to medium-high until the mixture turns white and soft peaks form that fold over when you lift the whisk up rather than staying stiff and formed. If you beat the egg whites until they

are stiff, it is harder to fold them evenly into the batter and you will have lumps of egg white throughout. Alternatively, you can beat it by hand with an egg whisk but this takes much longer and is hard work.

3. When using an electric jug blender, make sure the lid is on correctly before blending. You may need to scrape down the sides with a spatula and blend further to mix thoroughly. Remember to turn the electricity off at the wall switch before opening your electric appliances.

4. If you add the butter to the pan and it starts to foam and brown straight away, your pan is too hot and you need to turn the heat down. You want the butter to form yellow, foam-like bubbles that smell delicious, not burnt. If you pour your pancake batter quickly, this will also help to lower the pan's temperature.

FRENCH TOAST

French toast is so easy, and it is something I used to make as a kid. It's a great way to use up bread that might be past its best. If the last few slices of a loaf are not that fresh, pop them in the freezer to use later for French toast. I will then defrost them in the frypan while the pan is warming up and I get out the other ingredients – eggs and butter.

One beaten egg is usually enough to coat one slice of

bread. Cut each slice of bread into quarters and dip into beaten egg before frying in a medium pan of melted foaming butter.

Turn when one side is golden and partly crispy, adding more butter to the pan if needed. When both sides are cooked, remove from the pan and eat while warm.

These are good enough to eat plain without adding the empty calories of sugar or other toppings. When serving, you can sprinkle lightly with ground cinnamon.

You can also add other ingredients to the beaten egg mixture such as ground cinnamon, a sprinkle of icing sugar, vanilla seeds, essence or paste, and a splash of milk to thin the mixture slightly.

French toast can be an excellent way to get children to eat brown bread. You can also try using brioche, which is sweeter and richer than standard bread. It is also lighter, so it will absorb more egg mixture and require longer cooking times on a lower heat to thoroughly cook the egg without burning the outside.

Tip: When dipping the bread in the egg mixture, don't leave it to soak, especially brioche, or it will absorb too much mixture and you will end up with an uncooked, eggy centre.

MUESLI

Mixing your own muesli is cheaper and healthier than buying it. Shop-bought muesli is quite expensive, especially when sold in small quantities, and it often has surprising amounts of sugar.

Buying the individual ingredients in bulk and then mixing the quantities to your taste can result in considerable savings over time. Use traditional rolled oats rather than 'quick' porridge oats. Oats are a great source of fibre, antioxidants and slow-release carbohydrates.

Here is a list of what I add to traditional rolled oats:

- Goji berries
- Cacao nibs or powder
- Linseeds
- Sunflower seeds
- Pumpkin seeds (pepitas)
- Dried cranberries
- Hemp seeds
- Psyllium husks
- Acai powder

This is a great way to be healthy and creative, tailoring the proportions to your tastes, varying the ingredients and amounts each time. These ingredients are great pantry items to have on hand to add to baking – see the Healthy slice recipe on page 115.

BIRCHER MUESLI

It only takes a little extra planning the night before to make Bircher muesli and it will last about three days in the fridge, so it can be ready to go if you are pressed for time in the morning.

You want roughly double the quantity of liquid to oats. You can just use milk for your liquid or you can substitute part of it for yoghurt and/or orange or apple juice. I would still keep at least half of the total liquid quantity milk. You can use various milk types: skim, full cream, soy or almond milk.

I like to soak sultanas in orange juice before adding them, so they are extra plump and juicy. Honey is a great natural sweetener to add and the unique flavour of a locally sourced product comes through. Add ground cinnamon for spice. You can also add chopped nuts and any of the ingredients in the previous Muesli recipe. Mix through some freshly grated apple or other fresh fruit before serving.

CHIA PUDDING

This is an excellent alternative to Bircher muesli. Chia seeds are so rich in nutrients and low in calories that they are often referred to as a 'superfood'. Chia seeds absorb liquid to swell to about 10 times their weight, so you want to soak them before you eat them and a small amount goes a long way. (Don't eat the dry seeds, especially in large quantities, as they will absorb water and swell in your gut, causing digestive problems and abdominal pain.)

Ingredients: For a quarter of a cup of chia seeds, you want to add about 1 cup of yoghurt and 1 cup of milk. I like to use a good-quality, low-fat, no-added-sugar, vanilla Greek yoghurt. Part of the milk quantity can be substituted for maple syrup and vanilla essence; vary the quantities to suit your taste. For example, instead of 250ml milk, try 200ml milk, 40ml maple syrup and 10ml vanilla essence. You can increase the amount of maple syrup to add sweetness.

Method: Place all the ingredients in a bowl with a pinch of salt and hand whisk with a balloon whisk to aerate and produce an even mixture. Pour into individual serving dishes or one big dish and set in the fridge overnight. It will keep in the fridge for up to 5 days. Serve with fresh fruit. This is so delicious it also works as a healthy dessert option.

WAFFLES

A waffle maker can be a great item to put on your Christmas or birthday wish list. It means you can make an inexpensive 'special' breakfast at home instead of eating out or buying pre-made or frozen waffles. Not only are you saving money, you can ensure you are eating fresh ingredients and you have more control over the sugar and salt content. They are great fun to make, easy enough for kids to master and fill your kitchen with the smell of freshly baked waffles.

We just follow the basic recipe that came with the waffle

maker. I prefer to use a recipe with buttermilk, egg and self-raising flour (or plain flour and baking powder) rather than yeast. I don't follow the recipe instructions for the method of combining the ingredients. I just put all the ingredients directly into the electric mixer bowl. I sit the bowl on the kitchen scale and re-zero the scale after adding each ingredient, which saves on washing-up. Don't over-mix the waffle mixture; just bring everything together. It doesn't matter if the mixture is lumpy.

CRÊPES

A crêpe is basically a large, very thin pancake. There is something delicious about fresh crêpes with crispy edges, cooked in foaming butter. They are best eaten straight away, often straight from the pan, without even making it to the table.

They are so good I recommend you try them plain first. Lemon and sugar is a classic topping, but once your palate has had this much sugar you won't be able to appreciate the flavours of the plain crêpe. Not having any toppings also reduces the calories.

I have never seen the value in crêpe makers as crêpes are so easy to make in a frying pan.

The equipment: Investing in a good-quality non-stick frypan that is just the right size for one crêpe is useful and it can be used for many other dishes, such as omelettes. Keep this pan in good condition; never use any utensils that might scratch the non-stick surface. I make sure no-one uses my crêpe pan for any cooking that might damage it.

The batter: When you start out making crêpes, work out how much batter you will need to thinly cover the bottom of your pan. I use a 24cm pan and add one soup ladle, which holds about a quarter of a cup, or 60ml batter, per crêpe. For every 300ml milk (I use skim), add 1 cup of flour (130g), 1 egg and 1 tablespoon of caster sugar. It is that simple!

Step 1: Make the batter. I add all the ingredients straight into the electric jug blender on the scale and zero the scale after adding each one. I find that by adding the liquid ingredients (milk and eggs) before the dry ingredients (flour and caster sugar), you avoid clumps of dry ingredients forming in the bottom of the jug. You only need a few pulses for a smooth batter. Don't over-mix it. I let the batter sit for half an hour, then stir through half a ladle of water before making the crêpes.

Step 2: Evenly heat the pan on a medium heat before you start, so the butter foams when you add it but doesn't brown. Pick up the pan and swirl it to evenly distribute the butter over the pan surface. (If the pan seems too hot and the butter instantly foams and sizzles, quickly take the pan off the heat and add your batter as described in the next step, which will help cool it down. Then adjust your heat setting and return the pan to the lower heat.)

Step 3: Add one soup ladle of batter and tilt the pan so the mixture thinly coats the bottom of the pan. Once the batter looks like it is set, you can flip the crêpe. Use a spatula to lift the edge to check it is cooked underneath before flipping. It doesn't take long to cook each side, so you have to stay by the pan. If you get distracted, before you know it, it will burn. If you flip it before the batter is set, the batter will splash and the crêpe will be harder to flip and fold or break.

After flipping the crêpe, cook until the underneath is golden brown. Transfer to a plate and cover while you add the next one. These are usually eaten as fast as I can cook them.

I add a very small amount of butter to the pan between cooking each crêpe. Each time, I wait for the butter to foam before adding more batter. I like using salted butter and I therefore don't add salt or butter to the crêpe batter. The butter on the outside is what makes them so delicious.

If it is at all possible for there to be any leftover crêpes, they freeze well. Place non-stick wrap or paper between each one.

You can then heat them straight from the freezer in the microwave or in your non-stick crêpe pan. There is no need to add any more butter to the pan.

PART FIVE

LUNCHES, LUNCH BOXES & SNACKS

Children shouldn't leave home without knowing how to cook. Or worse, they won't leave home if they can't cook.

We rarely sit down to a cooked lunch, except at Christmas. I am usually too busy at work to stop for lunch and on weekends, a late breakfast means we are usually not hungry until dinner. An early dinner also means you don't go to bed on a full stomach. I only eat lunch if I am hungry. This should be true for any meal. For those people watching their weight, why eat a meal when you're not hungry just because it is considered a 'mealtime'?

Snacks

If I start to feel peckish, a small, healthy snack can often tide me over until dinner and learning to not always respond to hunger can help with weight control. Sometimes just a carrot, a piece of fruit, some yoghurt, a glass of milk, a juice or a coffee may be enough. Nuts, crackers, biscuits or popcorn, although excellent, can be moreish and harder to portion control. They can be easier to control if you take a portion with you to work.

With small children, we usually pack snacks and water or other drinks when leaving the house. This saves money, avoids having to stop to find food or drink when we are out, especially as children don't usually want to wait very long to be served in a store if they are hungry or thirsty. This also avoids them being tempted in a shop by unhealthy foods or receiving oversized portions. Why don't we do the same for ourselves for all the same reasons? If you are trying to control your weight, taking a small amount of effort to pack a snack and drink for when you go out can help you avoid temptation and save dollars on incidental spending. Those dollars can add up over months and years.

Having snacks with me at work came from when I was consulting and running late and never got a lunch break. Keeping snacks in my handbag has allowed me to keep working at my desk and grab a bite between patients. I know this is not mindful eating and I should take more time out during my busy day. Five minutes of sunshine would be enjoyable and I aspire to this one day but I am still a work in progress. But every cloud has a silver lining. My overworking habits save me calories and dollars.

I prefer to graze on snacks not just for time management but to keep my brain focused, mainly during that mid-morning and mid-afternoon period. With a morning and afternoon snack, I may not need anything in the middle of the day. A more substantial lunch tends to slow my brain down and a mid-morning snack can stop me going for a sugar hit or overeating at lunchtime.

Popcorn is a great snack to take to work or school. It can be prepared quickly the night before in the microwave. A popcorn machine is inexpensive, spits out popcorn super-fast and it's fun to use. If it means the kids will make the popcorn, it might be worth the investment. It might be an ideal birthday or Christmas present. Not only is it better when made fresh, it is much cheaper to buy the popcorn kernels than a packet of popped corn.

Drinking water and herbal tea throughout the day helps me to keep hunger at bay and limit calories.

SCHOOL LUNCHES

School lunches are a significant stress in my life. I find deciding what to make is much harder than actually making a school lunch, so I have shared with you my ideas. What is there that is easy to prepare (by you or preferably by them), that your child will actually eat and will stay fresh in the Australian climate at school until lunchtime, without refrigeration? If you look at safe food standards, not much is considered OK for consumption without refrigeration for over four hours in our summers. You are lucky if your school's "healthy choices" lunch orders are genuinely healthy and delicious enough for a child to prefer them to the unhealthy options on offer at the school tuckshop or canteen. If you are buying lunch orders for children at school or buying your lunch every day at work, you could be saving big money by taking food from home instead.

Sandwiches

Sandwiches are the classic school or work lunch solution. Frozen sandwiches, individually wrapped, easily defrost by lunchtime in Australia. The bread is less likely to be soggy or dry when frozen and less time spent at room temperature is better for food safety. Cooked meat freezes well, including leftover turkey, roast chicken or beef and slow-cooked pork, lamb or beef. You can make large portions for a weekend dinner, then finely chop the leftover cooked meat, after removing any fat, and freeze. The cooked meat is then on hand for sandwiches, just add any sauces, mustards or other spreads.

I sometimes make a batch of sandwiches on the weekend and freeze them to save time on weekday mornings when getting out the door for work and school drop-off can be challenging. Somehow, cutting the crusts off and cutting the sandwiches into squares makes them look more refined and appealing – think high tea. Don't throw out the crusts. These can be left to partly dry out and used to make breadcrumbs or fried crusts (see page 60).

Individually wrap sandwiches before freezing. To avoid having soggy bread by lunchtime, you don't want too much liquid in your filling. A good spread of butter helps stop moisture getting into the bread.

Some sandwich suggestions:

- Roast chicken, finely chopped, with finely chopped celery and chopped peanuts. Add just enough mayonnaise to bind together. Don't add so much mayonnaise that you can see it pooling in the bowl or between the ingredients, as the flavour will be overpowering and it will make the bread soggy. Season to taste with sea salt and cracked pepper. To save time, you can use a shop-bought roast chicken breast. One chicken breast will be enough for several sandwiches.

- Roast beef with seeded mustard or tomato chutney.

- Pulled pork with stewed apples. Apple sauce may make the bread soggy. A good spread of butter helps to prevent this. Stew apples gently in a pan with a little lemon juice so they are soft but still maintain their shape. This will mean less liquid is absorbed into the bread.

- Lamb with mint jelly or finely sliced fresh mint leaves.

- Curried egg: Hard-boil eggs and chop them up. To boil an egg, I put the cold egg from the fridge in cold water in a pan and bring to a rapid boil. Boil for 5 minutes. I find the egg is less likely to crack than if I add a cold egg to already boiling water. Remember to drain and let the egg cool before peeling it to avoid burning your fingers. Add enough mayonnaise to just bind together and enough curry powder to suit your taste. You may only need a teaspoon. Ideally, you should use one that's suited to a fish or vegetable curry. Use fresh, organic free-range eggs and good-quality whole-egg mayonnaise if possible.

You can also make sandwich fillings on the weekend and they will keep in the fridge for a few days. Other fresh ingredients can be added when the sandwich is made on the day, such as finely sliced lettuce or sprouts. Just make sure these are dried well after washing – a salad spinner works well. Alternatively, you can add fresh salad in the morning to a frozen sandwich from the freezer.

Other ideas

- Leftover cooked meat patties, burgers and sausages are another easy finger food on their own or they can be sliced for sandwich fillings.
- Roasted vegetables, such as pumpkin, carrot and potato, can be eaten at room temperature. See Roast vegetables (page 101).
- Cold meats such as ham or salami with dried fruit, nuts, cheese and crackers.
- Homemade hummus or other dips with crudités – carrot, celery and cucumber sticks, snow peas, sliced radish.

- Blanched vegetables like asparagus or beans can be prepared the night before.

Salads

Salads can be made the night before, refrigerated and then taken to school or work to eat at room temperature. Keep the salad dressing separate and add just before eating.

Tomato salad: A simple, fresh tomato salad can be prepared the night before as the tomato stews in the juices and the flavours develop. This is especially good if you have access to good-quality tomatoes. Slice or quarter the tomatoes and toss them in extra-virgin olive oil, balsamic vinegar, sea salt and pepper to taste. Add fresh basil leaves in the morning. For something more substantial, you can mix it with canned chickpeas (rinsed and drained).

Potato salad: Potato salad can also be prepared the night before and refrigerated overnight to eat at room temperature. Mix a dressing of extra-virgin olive oil, lemon juice, seeded mustard, finely chopped herbs, sea salt and cracked pepper to taste. For a quarter cup of oil, you might add a tablespoon each of mustard and lemon juice, but adjust the quantities to your taste. Whisk to combine with a fork. Boil the potatoes until soft when tested with a skewer but still a bit firm and not falling apart. Drain and cut into thick slices or pieces while hot. The pieces should be thick enough to hold their shape and not fall apart. Avoid burning your fingers by using tongs and a fork to pick up and hold the hot potato, then pour the dressing over the hot potatoes. Using baby or new potatoes saves time because you don't need to peel them and you can just cut them in half and add the dressing.

Biscuits

Having grown up with a mother and grandmother who were stay-at-home mums who usually baked daily has meant baking is a routine part of my week, although it's mostly confined to Sundays. Sunday morning is usually spent making a cooked breakfast, making bread in the breadmaker and baking for the school week's recess. I have found biscuits and slices keep better than cakes or muffins and usually last until Friday.

Biscuits are often better if the dough is refrigerated for a couple of hours before cutting into biscuits and baking. This flexibility to make biscuits in two stages suits my busy schedule. I can make the dough the day before and refrigerate overnight. Even better, I'll make double the recipe and roll a batch into a log, wrap it in cling wrap and freeze. This stash of dough in the freezer allows me to have homemade, fresh biscuits in minutes. The log can be cut frozen, usually six biscuits per baking tray, and often takes only 10-15 minutes to bake. Baking time varies depending on whether the dough is frozen, how thick the biscuits are, the type of mixture and your oven. I can usually tell when the baking is done by the smell. It is that yummy, freshly baked smell (the one you get just before the burnt smell).

The other advantage of having logs of dough on hand in the freezer is the ability to make small batches, so 12 instead of 24 biscuits at a time. This might be for portion control or because you are baking for only one or two people. If I know my son will take three biscuits for recess for five days in a week, then I only bake 15 biscuits for the week, which stops me from eating them. Even home-baked biscuits should be consumed in moderation. Home-baked biscuits taste so good, my son will rarely eat shop-bought biscuits. For a basic biscuit recipe, see Biscuits (page 109).

Toasted sandwiches

Toasted sandwiches are a great idea for a quick lunch at home.

Ham and cheese toastie: Ham and cheese is a classic and tastes great made in the frypan. We usually keep some sliced homemade bread in the freezer. I take out two slices and place in a large frypan on a medium-to-low heat. This helps to defrost the bread while I get the ham and butter out of the fridge. Cheese has a long life in the fridge so it's also a great go-to snack a week or so after your last shopping trip. Ham can also be stored sliced in the freezer. Place non-stick wrap between the ham slices. It will defrost quickly when laid out. If I am organised, I will take it out to defrost, but if I forget I will just cook the sandwich longer in the frypan at a lower heat. I like to butter one side of the bread and fry this first, which will defrost frozen bread. I then turn it over and use this side for the inside of my sandwich, adding the ham, sauce or mustard, and cheese. I then place the second piece of bread on top, butter the outside and fry. Turn the sandwich carefully to cook the other side. Hold it together with tongs and a turner.

Sandwich-maker toasties: A sandwich toaster or jaffle iron seals the edges, allowing you to use more liquid ingredients. This can be a great way to use up leftovers like bolognese, savoury mince, tuna mornay, curry, risotto, casserole and more. When filling the sandwiches, use less of the liquid sauce. Follow the machine instructions regarding quantities as only small amounts are required to fill each section. They are great fun to use and easy for children to manage with care if they are old enough.

INDEX

D

E

F

G

H

Ham chicken stew: 71-72; sandwiches: 146; toasted sandwiches 149-150

Healthy slice 115, 132

Herbs (dry, fresh) 13, 19, 31, 34, 41; poaching fish: 50; bolognese: 56; with vegetables: 60; risotto: 62; ragu: 78; pasta: 87; roast: 97-98; stock: 105; scrambled eggs: 126; potato salad: 147

L

Lamb shoulder (slow-cooker) 89

Lemon (juice, seed, wedges) 10, 45-48, 49-50, 64, 67, 68, 69, 73, 89, 91, 92, 93, 97, 98; zest: 31, 44, 47, 67-69, 73, 91-92; fish cakes: 44-45; fish fillets: 46-48; pasta: 49; poaching fish: 50; risotto: 64, 67-69, 92-93; chicken stew: 73; fritter mix: 91; dipping sauce: 92; roast: 97; gravy: 99; stock: 105; biscuits: 110, 112; apple crumble: 118; crêpes: 135; sandwiches: 145; potato salad: 147

Lemon-chicken risotto (*see also* Chicken) 92

Lemongrass 38, 48, 86

M

Meat and veg 57

Mince, beef 33, 51, 52-54, 55, 56, 57, 150
  Pasta Bolognese 54-55
  Savoury mince 51

Muesli 131, 133
  Bircher muesli 132

Mushroom risotto 151

N

Nuts (fresh, roasted, toasted) chestnuts: 39, 83; peanuts: 41, 81, 82, 112, 117, 145; cashews: 41, 94, 96; pine nuts: 67, 68, 88, 94

Nuts (ingredients for) stir-fry: 39-40; risotto: 67-68; fried rice: 81-83; pesto: 88; gnocchi: 94; curries: 94, 96; biscuits: 112; healthy slice: 115; biscuit base: 117; ganache: 119; bircher muesli: 133; snacks: 141; sandwiches: 145-146

P

R

S

T

V

W

CPSIA information can be obtained
at www.ICGtesting.com
Printed in the USA
BVHW041834081221
623566BV00014B/827